ANTELOPE COUNTRY

PRONGHORNS:
THE LAST AMERICANS

Published by

krause publications

700 E. State St. • Iola, WI 54990-0001

Please call or write for a free catalog of publications. The toll-free number to place
an order or to request a free catalog is (800) 258-0929, or use our regular
business number (715) 445-2214.
Library of Congress Catalog Number: 2001086365
ISBN: 0-87349-279-X
Printed in Canada

To those who cared for pronghorns and brought them back.
— *Valerius Geist*

To my wife, Victoria, and daughters, Elizabeth and Emily
— *Michael Francis*

A TERRITORIAL, EAR-TAGGED BUCK with his ear-tagged harem on the National Bison Range in Montana. Ear-tagging allows researchers to follow an antelope through the seasons and over the years.

CONTENTS

FOREWORD

Several years ago, I was trapped in the back of a small commuter prop-jet traveling to Charlottesville, Va., for a three-day conference on white-tailed deer. Judging by the conversation of several passengers around me, it was obvious they were agency biologists and/or wildlife professors who couldn't wait until the conference to talk shop.

I felt safe in my anonymity, and didn't hint that I was eavesdropping. As these professionals shared ideas on deer and the social issues surrounding high whitetail populations, I noticed a distinguished-looking man also eavesdropping. It was obvious he was listening, because he smiled occasionally and nodded his head in agreement when particular comments were heard above the prop-jet's drone.

The next evening, I walked into the hotel's conference room and took a seat near the front to hear a debate on elk ranching. The talks would pit an elk-ranch industry spokesman against a legendary wildlife professor from Calgary named Valerius Geist. When I was seated, I noticed my fellow eavesdropper from the day before. He was talking with the moderator and a few others near the podium. I was close enough to detect his Germanic accent.

Suddenly, recognition flashed through my brain. My "fellow eavesdropper" was Valerius Geist! (Forehead smack!) I had shared an airplane ride and ridden alone to the hotel, when I could have introduced myself and shared some time with this friendly, agreeable man. For several years, I had admired him from afar. I had been awed by his writings against elk ranching, and admired how he eloquently battled this and other threats to North America's phenomenal system of wildlife management.

Fortunately, I've found opportunity to work with Geist and learn much from him since. Still, I'll never forget the valuable lesson he taught me during that flight to Charlottesville — without saying a word. Geist likely knew more about the issues being discussed than anyone on that plane, but he stayed quiet and listened, appreciating what he heard but content to sit quietly. Or maybe he is humble enough to know he can still learn as a silent observer.

Or maybe Geist just enjoys hearing a good story. He certainly enjoys telling one. Not only is he a well-schooled researcher in animal behavior, but he knows how to communicate. He masterfully combines biology, history, politics and archaeology to explain the wild world around us.

Antelope Country demonstrates Geist's storytelling skills. He takes rich examples from science, history and culture, and weaves them into a fascinating account of the pronghorn's unique place in North America.

Complementing Geist's text is the dramatic camera work of Michael Francis, whose photographs illustrate the pronghorn's obvious grace, as well as the prairie's subtle beauty. Francis plays off Geist's thoughts and provides the perfect exclamation point in his photography. If you've never stood on the Great Plains and watched pronghorns atop a distant rise, Geist and Francis inspire you to see it firsthand.

Geist also explains the pronghorn's miraculous survival from an era that preceded human presence in North America. How did the pronghorn live and flourish in a time when it shared its habitat with the largest predatory mammals to ever roam North America? What allowed the pronghorn to adapt to a modern-day prairie habitat that's vastly different from the one it knew before the ice ages? And which predator threatened and then saved the pronghorn from extinction in the past 100 years?

Geist and Francis explain and illustrate it all in *Antelope Country*, an entertaining, fast-paced account of a swift, beautiful creature. No other writers, scientists, photographers or social commentators could give this animal the appreciation it has earned. Somehow, Geist and Francis shoulder all four responsibilities with equal grace and skill.

— *Patrick Durkin, April 2001*

INTRODUCTION

The pronghorn is something special. It is a species with a stunning past that reflects itself in its structure, behavior and ecology. It not only raises the tragic specter that surrounds the last of its kind, but it also raises hope for the future, because the pronghorn survived into modern times despite daunting odds. Here is living proof of what goodwill, dedication and intellect can do in conservation and in repairing the Earth's biota. And it was all done without fanfare, without individuals or organizations clamoring for and bathing in the limelight. It is an example of what honest grass-root conservation can and does accomplish.

When I see bands of pronghorns on the open prairie, I not only thrill at their grace and beauty and at the insight into their lives, but I also reflect on what might have been had it not been for so many forgotten individuals, long covered by sod, who were determined that future generations should see the pronghorn. That makes my day, no matter what worries gnaw at my soul. Human decency can triumph, and human decency will triumph. Let's give it a chance in reversing the degradation of our planet. To me, the pronghorn is an image of hope and optimism, a testimony to North America's good side.

Ecologically, pronghorns functioned as prey, and their biology is an extreme case of defeating predation. They were part of the greater cycle of birth and death, of gathering nutrients and energy and passing it on when the circle closed. Pronghorn conservation was based on our participation in that circle. It meant not the preservation of a few individuals or even populations as examples of "natural art," but on spreading the species so that it might transform the harsh and daunting prairie into sustenance for us, so that we might be part of that greater cosmic cycle. Our friends who are native to this land saw sacredness in this. Not preservation for preserva-

tion's sake, but maintenance of a vibrant interaction of man and prey in a dynamic system made conscious by our presence. Painfully conscious, I might add. The repair of Earth's biota can succeed only if we integrate ourselves into that greater circle of being, so that what we conserve literally becomes living matter within us.

In that context, we are reminded by our native friends that the taking of life is sacred. It is worthy of reflection as it makes us actors in fostering and in taking life, without which we could not live. Thus, I not only thrill at the sight of pronghorns, but also at the food they provide and all the family matters that were entailed in bringing such to the table. When cold autumnal winds sweep the prairie, I want to be out there with family and friends partaking in the wild harvest of tasting the very goodness of the Earth through the pronghorn, which my insights, skills and labor provided. I do not want to miss the adventures and companionship of the hunt, the thrill of the wild out there, the pronghorn, even though I might return empty-handed, as I have done on occasion. When I return with prey, it is always with wonder, a wonder shared by family and friends. It made pronghorns much more than pretty, interesting things running somewhere out there. It made them part of my physical being. Through hunting, I have become part pronghorn. I have consciously lived the great cycle.

It might be a personal weakness, but I cannot live without wanting to know. Idle curiosity, maybe, but it's an ingredient without which actions for the future cannot be formulated. Being prepared always requires understanding, and in that spirit I wrote this book. I am motivated by wonder, of which the pronghorn generated so very much for me. Maybe, just maybe, one can pass on a little of it.

— Val Geist, 2001

CHAPTER 1

A SURVIVOR FROM THOSE GLORIOUS DAYS

The prairies are a big piece of real estate. This is a land that stretches in endless expanses, where great buffalo herds once roamed, and the grasses teemed with wildlife. The pronghorn is the only large mammal left from those glorious days.

W est of the great Mississippi River stretches the dry interior of North America. Here are the prairies, first the tall-grass prairie of the lowlands of the East that gives way to the short-grass prairies of the center that merges into the grassy foothills of the Rockies. To the north, the prairie fades in Canada into aspen groves and boreal forests of Alberta and Saskatchewan; to the south it changes into America's unique deserts, reaching deep into Mexico. There is a big piece of real estate here between those boundaries to the north, south, east and west. This is the land where once the great buffalo herds roamed, where mounted Indian warriors made their last successful stands against the United States cavalry, as in Red Cloud's war over the Bozeman Trail or Custer's defeat at the Battle of the Little Bighorn. To the north, in Canadian territory, the Riel Rebellion of Metis and Indian people ran its tragic course. Here red-coated mounted police looked after law and order in the name of the British Crown. The mounted

WATER IS ESSENTIAL for pronghorns to survive. They will live in deserts, but only with adequate access to water.

This is a land of

G

natural grandeur

GRANDEUR

men in blue and red and their able adversaries now belong to history. The land has been civilized, and its primordial wildness replaced by cattle and cowboys, by big ranches and Indian reservations, by fields of wheat, barley, corn, sugar beets and alfalfa, by towering grain elevators and small, bustling towns, and by straight, broad interstate or interprovincial highways.

This is a land of natural grandeur. Here the view stretches forever. A wide sky arches over it all, infinitely blue in sunshine, garishly colored in flaming red at sunsets, and delicately painted in pink and blue pastel during quiet sunrises. And then there are the clouds. And what clouds! High clouds, low clouds, thin clouds, thick clouds, white clouds, black clouds, ever-changing clouds. Here you can watch dark thunderstorms form before your eyes, see them march past, spewing lightning, hail, rain and chilling wind gusts, while the very earth seems to shake with thunder. Tornadoes may claw at the earth. Here you can see the Northern lights at night overhead, usually

S U N L I

Here, winter days are clear and cold
with a thin sunlight tha

as moving green ribbons, but occasionally in full rainbow colors. Here the ground may be hard when dry but bottomless mud when wet.

Here Arctic air may lock the land in ice and silence. Here winter days are clear and cold with a thin sunlight that fails to warm, while at nights a big, bright moon hovers over the white landscape. Sudden snowstorms may bury you, as may blizzards, the ferocity of which mere words cannot describe. Nothing but frozen waste under a dark, lead-gray winter sky may meet your eyes, and yet this very land will be bright, flushed in vivid green, and teeming with life in spring and summer. Big ice floes scour the rivers at breakup, and once transported thousands of drowned buffalo and elk downriver, to the delight of native people who relished the cold-fermented meat.

Potholes rimmed by reeds were then and now the continent's waterfowl and shorebird factories. Myriad species of ducks, geese, swans, grebes, shorebirds and songbirds move to the prairie lakes and sloughs. Each dawn is alive with bird song. Sage grouse, sharp-tailed grouse and prairie chickens boom and display on their mating grounds. Mule deer and white-tailed deer feed below the towering badlands in coulees and along rivers. When spring comes, when the hills turn green, when life is rich and bubbling, then it's a time when one wishes to live forever. The bald prairie can be so gripping, so rich, and so beautiful. Extremes in climate and landscape is what the West is all about. Despite its seasonal harshness, it is an appealing land.

MILES AND MILES of fence lines now crisscross the West, and that's a bane to the pronghorn. Pronghorns are much impeded by fences. In fact, early native hunters built fences to herd pronghorn into corrals where they were captured.

One summer, many years ago, I flew from Washington, D.C., to Billings, Mont. I had suffered the heat and humidity of the East. When I stepped from the aircraft's door onto the open ramp and inhaled the Montana air, I froze in place. Heavens, what air! Cool. Dry. Delicious. At that moment, all I wanted to do was stand and breathe. Nothing else mattered. I was overwhelmed by that air, that wonderful Montana air. A shuffle behind me reminded me that I was blocking the exit in my rapture over breathing. Reluctantly, I gathered my wits and moved on. I remember to this day how that air awoke every cell in my body, how it thrilled every nook and cranny of my being. That's part of the great American West.

Much of the prairie land is tame now and much in human use. Rusty barbwire fences follow the roads. Beef cattle graze the pastures. Huge wheatfields stretch forever over the land. Tall grain elevators poke into the sky. Small-town America is at home here, hubs of commerce for the folks who raise cattle, grow wheat, dig oil wells, work the mines, keep the country going. Dilapidated it may be here and there, but one senses that all this commercial hustle and bustle is still young. The prairie does not have the "lived-in" look of Europe.

Before the old prairie trails were plowed under, this was the land of the Wild West of Charley Russell; of Sitting Bull, Red Cloud and the great Crazy Horse; of Hudson Bay traders and the Metis; of the Oregon Trail and aborted Bozeman Trail; of mountain men and smoke-spewing paddle wheel steamers and railways. This is the land of the great American romance with the West, of Billy the Kid, Buffalo Bill, Wyatt Earp and the shootout at the OK Corral. This is the heartland of the pronghorn, the buffalo's little brother, the last of the Americans.

The pronghorn, *Antilocapra americana Ord*, 1818, is also called pronghorn antelope, and, colloquially, simply antelope. And it is an antelope in everything but genetics. Genetically, the pronghorn is not an antelope, but the very last of an old all-American family of ruminants, or cud chewers. I shall refer to it here simply as pronghorn. It is also the last species of American large mammals that lived on the prairie to survive the great extinction that befell North America's big creatures at the end of the last ice age. It is truly the last of the Americans. Without the pronghorn, the open prairie would today be without a plains-adapted big-game species. The buffalo, after all, went over a century ago, and it is largely a Siberian by origin, not an old

SUDDEN WEATHER CHANGES mark the pronghorn's habitat. Pronghorns are discomforted by the sharp chill, which by tomorrow might change to blistering summer heat.

it is an appealing land

H E A R T L

This is the heartland of the pronghorn,
the last of the

A N D

Americans

American. While early European travelers saw and commented on pronghorns, first by Spaniards in Mexico who called it berrendo, it was not till the beginning of the 19th century that the famous Lewis and Clark expedition collected the first specimen of pronghorns for science. These gifted explorers called it an antelope. French-Canadian explorers labeled it cabrie, or kid. Native tribes had many names for it, of which more than 20 are known.

The great extinction began more than 10,000 years ago, just when people began to colonize this continent. The prairie they saw was very different then. To begin with, it was not bald, but a rich grassland studded by shrubs and trees. There were huge, tall-legged elephants with big curving tusks roaming in herds. There were myriad horses of different species, as well as guanacos, camels, long-horned bison and huge, peculiar ground sloths. Hunting them were lions, cheetahs, saber-tooth and dirk-toothed tigers, huge dire wolves and enormous, swift-footed predacious bears. It was a different world then, of which the pronghorn and its two four-horned relatives were an integral part.

By the time humans came, the American cheetah and the huge predacious bears were rare or had already died out along with several large herbivore species. Within a few thousand years, the bulk of species vanished. Today, the pronghorn is the only larger mammal left from those glorious days, when American plains teemed with more species of wildlife than did the African plains —

THE PRONGHORN AND WHITE-TAILED DEER (above) are both old Americans, both great survivors and both an unparalleled conservation success. Water holes, natural or man-made, are a necessity for pronghorns (left).

although the clever coyote was then present, too. Well, he would be!

While most pronghorns were found historically in the prairies east of the Rockies, they penetrated west as far as the central valleys of California and to Baja California, something the buffalo failed to accomplish post-glacially. Pronghorns occupied southwestern Oregon, southern Idaho, Nevada and south into western Texas and south of the Rio Grande deep into Mexico. Their easternmost distribution was in South Dakota and Nebraska. Pronghorns preferred, by all appearances, the short-grass prairie and semideserts where tall grass was uncommon and thus no obstacle to speedy flight.

Pronghorns released in Hawaii clung to closely cropped horse and cattle pastures and jumped about helplessly in the tall grass of ungrazed pastures. Pronghorns are also limited by scarcity of water. They are not true desert creatures. During summer they require about 3½ quarts of water per day. They do best on well-watered ranges.

Pronghorns are neither large nor fat. Adult females provide about 40 pounds of lean meat and bucks about 50 pounds. Fat was treasured by native people. Yet hunting pronghorns was considered worth the effort by even the earliest of hunters on this continent. When people colonized

central North America beginning about 11,500 years ago, they focused their hunting effort on the most profitable prey species: first on elephants and when these were gone, on the large, long-horned bison. Early archaeological sites of elephant hunters are labeled Clovis sites, and the later sites of the buffalo hunters are called Folsom sites.

Both are characterized by exquisitely crafted stone spear points. Remains of butchered pronghorn are found in Clovis and Folsom sites. Clearly, the earliest of Paleoindian hunters had mastered the art of catching such. How they did it remains a mystery, because their spears appear to have been made for hand-held stabbing, not a weapon of choice to hit a small ungulate with lightning-fast reflexes. Later hunters, with bow and arrow, took advantage of the curiosity of pronghorns to lure them into shooting distance or ambushed them at watering sites, hiding behind stone blinds. Today modern bow-hunters may use these very blinds. The chipped arrowheads found about such watering sites are mute evidence of shots missed in prehistory. In later millennia and right into the last century, pronghorns were apparently hunted communally by native bands. They were skillfully maneuvered into rather large and elaborate corrals made of juniper trees and sage brush that took a lot of time, effort and sophisticated knowledge to build. These corrals took

WYOMING EXHIBITS TYPICAL pronghorn prairie habitat: open spaces, wide vistas, grasslands, sage brush and old fields.

The
Pl

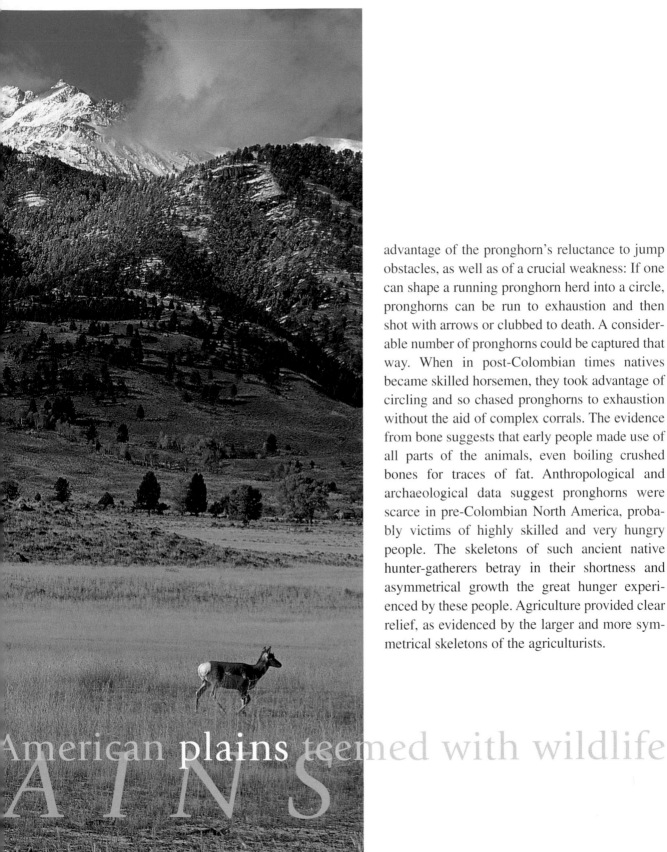

advantage of the pronghorn's reluctance to jump obstacles, as well as of a crucial weakness: If one can shape a running pronghorn herd into a circle, pronghorns can be run to exhaustion and then shot with arrows or clubbed to death. A considerable number of pronghorns could be captured that way. When in post-Colombian times natives became skilled horsemen, they took advantage of circling and so chased pronghorns to exhaustion without the aid of complex corrals. The evidence from bone suggests that early people made use of all parts of the animals, even boiling crushed bones for traces of fat. Anthropological and archaeological data suggest pronghorns were scarce in pre-Colombian North America, probably victims of highly skilled and very hungry people. The skeletons of such ancient native hunter-gatherers betray in their shortness and asymmetrical growth the great hunger experienced by these people. Agriculture provided clear relief, as evidenced by the larger and more symmetrical skeletons of the agriculturists.

American plains teemed with wildlife
AINS

Pronghorns would not be on the prairies today were it not for human effort. It required sacrifice, cooperation and care, beginning three generations ago, to bring them back. The pronghorn was then close to extinction, a victim of market hunting, but also of military policy that sought to deprive the last native people of their sustenance, so as to make them surrender, to accept life on reservations. The pronghorn is thus a species returned deliberately from the edge of extinction. It is a species whose existence advertises — nay, shouts loud and clear — that conservation works. Conservation also pays handsomely with hard dollars, jobs and commerce, and the pronghorn has returned many times over whatever favor we extended it.

The pronghorn, like all North American wildlife, is wildlife restored. It is here today not because of divine grace, but because of hands-on management by fledgling wildlife departments and a large amount of selfless volunteering by members of wildlife conservation clubs. Some of the most heroic efforts to save pronghorns were by concerned, civic-minded landowners. To these, in particular, we all owe a vote of thanks. The pronghorn is now abundant because we made it so. The pronghorn's fate today cannot be separated from human fate. Today the pronghorn stands as a symbol to much that is good and decent in North America.

PRONGHORNS LIKE FLAT, unobstructed terrain for running (below). A mature buck is an antelope in all its heredity (right). Genetically, this is a unique ruminant, one purely of American descent, the last survivor of a venerable lineage.

CHAPTER 2

ARMED FOR DEFENSE

A pronghorn's eyes are wide-set
and enormous, revealing its incredible
eyesight. Those eyes scan the plains
and keep watch over the skies.
When trouble is detected, they run,
skimming the ground with head held
high in search of opportunities.

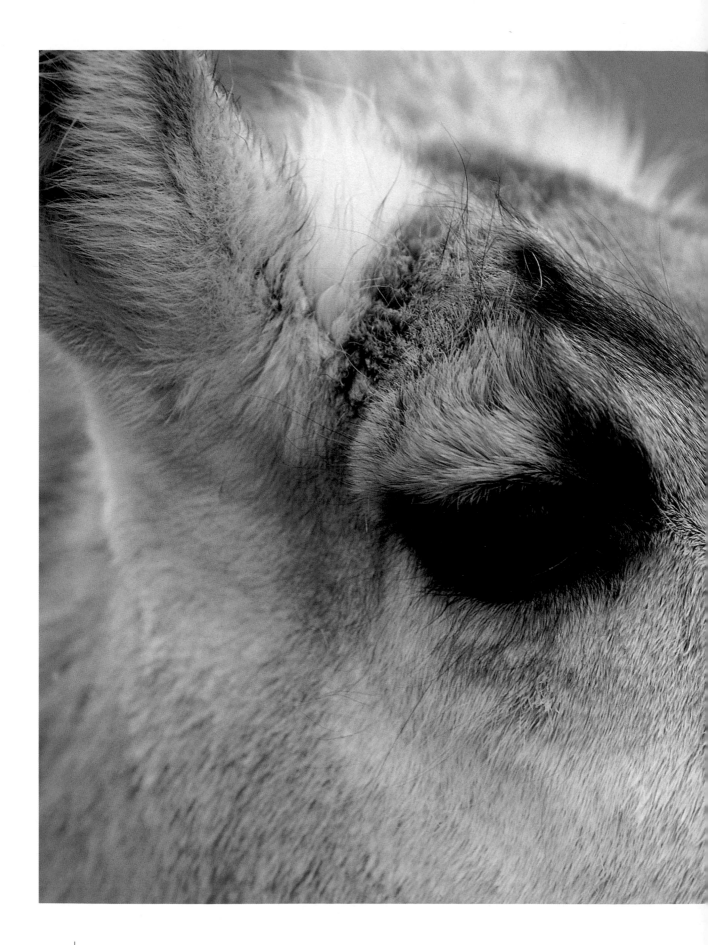

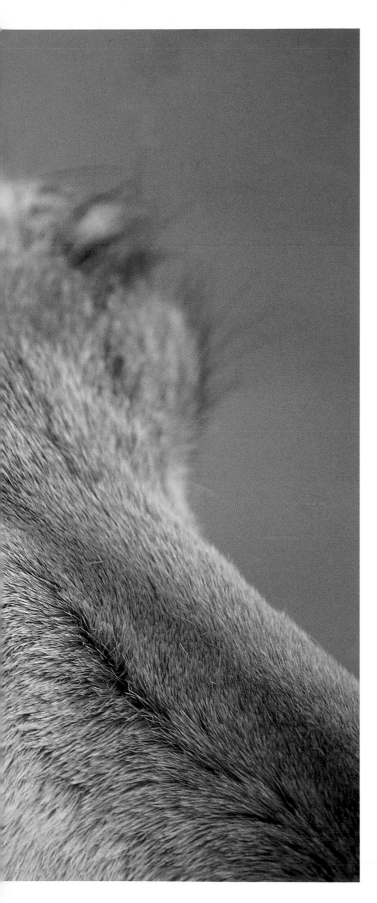

The eyes of the pronghorn are a puzzle. They are larger than those of an elephant. They match in size the eyes of a horse, which has the largest eyes among four-legged beasts. The bony orbits of a pronghorn's skull are huge and engulf the eyes, together with their associated muscles and fat padding, so that one must chip away the bone to extract an eye undamaged. The orbits are largest in their vertical dimension, as if allowing the eye some movement up and down to see better in the sky above. And that was indeed necessary, for unlike today's skies, those of the past ice ages in North America were filled with many species of huge, but now extinct, birds of prey. The pronghorn's eyes are heavily pigmented. That is, they are very dark in color, much as in other plains-dwellers that must deal with intense sunlight from above in summer and with equally dazzling light reflected from the snow blanket in winter. Long, black eyelashes do their part to shade the eyes from the sun.

Why such huge eyes on the pronghorn? No plains-dwelling antelope from Africa or Asia has eyes as large as the pronghorn's. What natural selection drove the evolution of so huge an eye? Why was the performance evolved by Old World antelopes not good enough for pronghorns?

PRONGHORN EYES are wide-set and enormous in size for so small-bodied an antelope. Dark pigments and long, black eyelashes protect the sensitive eye from the glare of the sun or from sunlight reflected on the snow. Pronghorns live by their eyes, whose acuity is legendary.

What was it that extracted ever superior performance from the pronghorn's eyes? Clearly, pronghorns with smaller eyes failed to make the grade and were eliminated by natural selection for one reason or other. What might those reasons have been?

In the past, superior vision was, apparently, vital to the life of pronghorns. Superior vision, however, is not merely a matter of visual acuity, but also the ability to correctly identify danger from nondanger with speed and precision. We know pronghorns can be very curious, and may approach objects unknown to them from afar. They are attracted to the unknown, which they inspect. Thereafter, they may flee — or they may not. That is, pronghorns do not run off blindly from potential danger, but rather decipher what they have seen and flee only if needed.

This is an important point. African antelope are not renowned for this behavior, though some do practice it. Nor do African antelope tame as readily as pronghorns. To do so, pronghorns must be capable of readily distinguishing danger from nondanger and act logically and consistently on that distinction.

The ability of pronghorns to distinguish danger from nondanger is more than remarkable. In southern Alberta there is a large military base, Suffield, which is home to many pronghorns. It is a major tank and infantry training ground used by Canadian and European troops. My students and I had access to this base when doing research

IN ARCTIC COLD and blowing snow, when the wind chill is high, pronghorns lie down, facing downwind, below. A snow storm could almost bury them, but they are very cold hardy. While running, a pronghorn's hoofs barely clear the snow, right.

$WEATHER$

then kills pronghorns

BEAUT

They glanced up, scanned us with thos
beautiful eyes and went promptl

on deer and pronghorns. The base commander kindly drove me out on an inspection trip the first time we met. Pronghorns were scattered all about the prairie in small herds. We stopped repeatedly mere feet from them, but the pronghorns did not flee. They glanced up, scanned us with those dark, beautiful eyes of theirs and went promptly back to feeding. Clearly, soldiers in jeeps were neither a novelty nor a danger. Nor, for that matter, were live fire exercises by tanks, nor maneuvers by infantry on foot with fire support. The pronghorns merely stepped out of the way to let the armored behemoths and the soldiers pass. The commotion, the noise, the gunfire meant nothing. They had heard it all before and accepted it as part of their normal daily life.

Suffield is a wildlife jewel in the Canadian prairie, in good part a product of the care and concern of the officers and men operating this training base. Would you calmly stay and eat your meal with tanks hurtling past you but a few feet away, their cannons and machine guns ablaze? The pronghorns did just that. Pronghorns are smart!

How well do pronghorns see? We have no studies comparing the performance of the pronghorn's eyes with those of horses and Old World antelope. However, observations in the field indicate that pronghorns can detect and correctly respond to an enemy at unbelievable distances — provided the pronghorn is in distress. That is an important condition. Where pronghorns are used to people, their

PRONGHORNS WILL LOOK you over. They do not run blindly from all danger. They respond to predators selectively. Consequently, they soon learn not to flee from harmless humans. But, watch out after the first day of hunting season.

miraculous ability at spotting and correctly responding to danger remains, of course, concealed. To detect how well pronghorns can see requires danger.

It is no different with us. We do not know our aptitudes till tested under duress. I did not know, for instance, how well I could climb till a grizzly bear put me up a tree. With unbelievable speed, but above all, with great precision and unshakable confidence, I ascended a tall white spruce. For a moment I felt disembodied, as if outside myself and a mere spectator to the show. Reaching the top, I grabbed a branch with one hand and putting one foot against the trunk — to my utter amazement — I spread-eagled and screamed lustily at the grizzly far below. And these acrobatics were performed 50 feet or more above the ground.

In that frame of mind, height meant nothing to me. I was in euphoria, without the slightest fear. It was as if I had been transformed into an earlier ancestor, a tree-climbing one, which might not have been far off the true state of affairs. Later, when I examined the spruce tree with sober eyes, I was incredulous at what I had done.

In a similar vein, one cannot discover the phenomenal eyesight of a pronghorn unless the animal is trying desperately to escape. My first

experience with that was, consequently, not pretty. Early one opening day of antelope season, I saw a couple of fellows jump from a truck and open fire on a distant herd of pronghorns. The herd fled past me more than a half-mile away. Trailing the herd were two bucks, each with one front leg dangling. It was awful. The two shooters went back to their truck and drove off, making no attempt to follow. That was worse!

Indignant, I set off to get at least one of those wounded bucks. I saw one lie down about a mile away, so I ducked into a coulee and followed. The first time the buck spotted part of my head at more than 600 yards distance, he jumped to his legs and fled. When I next found him, he was about a mile away, scanning for me. Again he fled as I peeked over a ridge. Thereafter, no matter how well I tried to hide, he always spotted me. I could not approach closer than a half-mile, and eventually lost him from sight.

Consider, would you be able to see part of a human head from over a mile away, even with a

As pronghorns grew scarce, they become more and more SPOOKY

spooky

S

good pair of binoculars? It is difficult, I can assure you, although with 8-power binoculars of exceptional quality it can be done. Barely. A dear friend of mine, long-accustomed to hunting bighorn sheep in the Rockies, rated the vision of escaping pronghorns as distinctly superior.

Those are not scientific ways to determine visual acuity, but they give an inkling of the power of the pronghorn's vision. The huge eyes and miraculous vision must have come in handy at the turn of the century when pronghorns were rapidly being shot from the plains and in danger of going the way of the buffalo. Hunters then noted that as pronghorns grew scarce, they became more and more spooky, and more and more difficult to approach. That they survived at all the huge slaughter of wildlife might have been because of their incredible vision, but also because of their ability to intelligently decipher what was dangerous and what was not. Moreover, the pronghorn apparently has remarkable night vision, as pronghorns were clocked running at some 50 mph beside a highway on a dark night.

The huge eyes of the pronghorn, its miraculous vision, and its intelligent exploration suggest that these faculties are the result of severe selection by predators, but by predator species that no longer exist on Earth. Much of the anatomy and behavior of the pronghorn leads to the same conclusion: This species evolved — and prospered — with predators of such high skills and determination as we can only imagine, but no longer observe.

Look at the pronghorn's legs. They are more highly evolved for running than any African antelope legs. Antelope or gazelle adapted as runners from the plains of Africa or Asia. They have greatly reduced dew claws, but the pronghorn has none at all. Its dew claws evolved away entirely. That implies the stresses and strains on pronghorn legs in running exceeded those experienced by comparable antelope in the Old World. So do the large elastic pads under the pronghorn's hoofs. Dew claws have also been lost by the giraffe, an old plains dweller, and by two of three species of the grysbock (*Raphicerus*), tiny shrub-adapted African antelope. Why that is so is not evident.

Moreover, the body proportions and behavior of the pronghorn identify it as a "long-legged cursor." The last term is just a fancy scientific word for "runner." The above implies, of course, that there are also short-legged runners, as indeed there are. Short-legged runners have evolved to run with very high speed over even, level, unobstructed ground, where during each sprint cycle the hoofs need to clear the ground only by a tiny space. The less the lift of hoofs and body above the ground, the cheaper it is for the animal to run.

Lift happens to be about 13 times more costly than the same distance of horizontal travel. Because running is terribly expensive in energy, natural selection has worked miracles in making running as cheap as possible. Short-legged runners happen to run with the least body lift and,

invariably, have one leg on the ground during the sprint cycle. They evolved the cheapest manner of running fast. We do not have a good example in North America of a short-legged runner, but several Old World antelope and gazelles fit the bill, such as the saiga antelope of the Volga plains, the addax of the Sahara or the Gems buck of the southwestern African deserts.

Long legged cursors, however, evolved with a handicap, namely the need to scan and evaluate where to run in uneven, broken, rocky, hilly, obstacle-strewn terrain. They cannot wind up and go lickety-split down a level field, heedless of where to step, as can short-legged runners. They have to scan what's ahead and then place their legs skillfully around and about obstacles, lest they stumble and fall. With a predator in hot pursuit, there is normally no second chance after a stumble. Long life and success go to whomever places the legs with ruthless precision while going faster than the enemy behind.

PRONGHORNS TYPICALLY run with head held high, scanning the terrain ahead for obstacles and opportunities. Pronghorn tracks, below, reveal no dewclaws.

Long-legged runners often progress in huge horizontal leaps, with the body suspended well above ground. All long-legged cursors have not only long legs, but also long necks, and all run with their head held high. They can thus scan the runway that lies ahead from a high vantage point. The eyes of the pronghorn, however, are not only very large, but are also widely spaced. This, together with the elevated head during running, suggests superior ability at judging distances and angles. Moreover, the pronghorn can switch its mode of high-running — instantly — from transverse to rotary gallop, the only cursorial species known to this. A long-legged cursor thus runs with a handicap: It needs time to scan accurately what lies ahead and then adjust its escape route and its foot-fall pattern accordingly. Yet, despite this handicap, the pronghorn is faster than any antelope from Africa or Asia, short-legged or long-legged.

Unfortunately, there is much dispute about the top speed of pronghorns. I suspect some pronghorns in full flight might exceed 60 mph. I also suspect that one record, which indicated a burst of speed as high as 70 mph by a barren female pronghorn, is valid because it matches exactly the top speed of tame cheetahs timed on a race track. Cheetahs could maintain that speed, at best, for about 500 yards. Female pronghorn can run faster than bucks by about 10 mph. On very broken, obstacle-strewn terrain, pronghorns — understandably — run with reduced speed. Pronghorns easily outrun

excellent saddle horses, although on at least a few occasions, riders have caught up to pronghorns because pronghorns severely pushed might suddenly collapse. Unlike horses, pronghorns tire more readily and cannot maintain their phenomenal top speed for long. However, they appear able to run without much fatigue at a cruising speed of 35 to 40 mph. Nevertheless, native people hunting pronghorn from horseback had to use ruses to tire pronghorns, such as surrounding a herd and chasing it back and forth in a circle for hours. Even then, despite hard riding and skillful horsemanship, failures were common and hunting success low. All in all, pronghorns at least match cheetahs in speed. Better research might show someday that their top speed exceeds even that of cheetahs. Clearly, pronghorns, for all the handicaps of a long-legged cursor, are formidable racers.

Before getting carried away, let me offer a qualifier: Not all pronghorns are fast or enduring, not all pronghorns adjust readily to human disturbance, and not all pronghorns are lively and inquisitive. This is true only for very healthy and, above all, large-bodied, well-grown pronghorns that have access to abun-

AFTER BEING CHASED by bucks, this doe, right, is panting, sticking out a black tongue. Pronghorns have extra large windpipes and lungs to inhale oxygen and expel carbon dioxide, big hearts to rapidly pump blood and specialized mechanisms to cool the brain. Pronghorns are designed to run.

Long life an

E C I S I O N

success go to whomever
places the legs with ruthless precision

DEC

Northern pronghorns are frequently decimated by severe winters

MATED

dant high-quality nutrition. Agricultural animal scientists would call such pronghorns "high-plane," referring to their plane or level of nutrition. The obverse would be "low plane," that is, chronically undernourished individuals. More detailed investigations revealed that the genetic potential of mammals is so plastic that the same genome in a good environment generates a high-performance, luxury type individual whose biological function is to colonize.

Poor nutrition generates the obverse, an efficiency-type individual whose biological function is to stay put and do as well as it can with what little it has. We can label it a "maintenance phenotype," and the luxury type individual is called a "dispersal phenotype." The latter is lively, inquisitive, exploratory, assertive and far-roaming, and it has a high reproductive rate. The maintenance phenotype is not a high performer in anything, neither physically nor reproductively. However, because it reproduces less, and because reproduction is costly to an individual and ages it faster, the small, lethargic, low-performer tends to live longer than the high-performing individual.

Consequently, expect the large-bodied pronghorns so typical of Northern prairies to be quite different in performance from the small-bodied Southern prong-

DEATH IN THE BADLANDS. The skull, backbone and horn of a large buck who failed to survive the rut become sun-bleached.

horns from hot, dry deserts. This is a vital distinction. What Northern phenotypes can do, Southern phenotypes might not. Luxury-type individuals far outperform efficiency- or starvation-type individuals. Nor must one assume that efficiency-type pronghorns in the South will remain such when conditions change very favorably. Given superior forage, many small, dainty and spooky Southern pronghorns will become robust, large and bold; in no way different from their Northern cousins.

Furthermore, no matter how robust the luxury-type pronghorn, severe weather will wear it down to the point where it cannot run fast. In fact, when in severe decline, it no longer cares about running, or anything else for that matter. That state of affairs happens too often in the Northern prairie when severe cold and snowfall at first hamper, and then incapacitate or kill pronghorns. When pronghorns are weak, coyotes have a heyday. When hunting in family packs, coyotes very efficiently dispatch pronghorns weakened by cold and starvation. Consequently, Northern pronghorns are quite frequently decimated by severe winters. If they survive to spring, however, they have access to a long growing season and rich herbage. That allows them to bear large, survivable fawns and produce an abundance of rich milk. That allows the fawns to mature rapidly and grow to superior adult size.

Southern pronghorns do not face such severe winters, and where water and abundant native forage is present, they grow into specimens just

ARMED FOR DEFENSE | 45

as large as Northern pronghorns. In very arid regions, however, they might struggle with great heat and lack of moisture. As a result, they might experience only brief seasonal periods of abundant good food. Most of the time, their food is much less digestible than the food enjoyed by pronghorns farther north. Consequently, they will likely have fewer and smaller fawns, less milk or run out of milk sooner. The fawns will likely grow slowly into adulthood and remain small-bodied with low performance for life. In the deserts, some plants, such as tar brush, will be consumed in quantity when better food is scarce. This might even kill malnourished pronghorns. As good as they probably are at detoxifying forages, there are limits to what pronghorns can do.

L et us now return again to pronghorns and running. Let us look at the prairie surface pronghorns must run over. This surface might be covered in one season by dry sage scrub, cacti and bitter brush, with rocks protruding here and there between the many holes dug by badgers, prairie dogs and ground squirrels. All these obstacles are ever ready to trap the unwary. Then again, the once hard, dusty surface might turn into a yellow slick during snow melt or after heavy rains. Pronghorns might then slide about spread-legged with balls of mud and dry grass encasing their slender hoofs. Winter brings slick, frozen surfaces, hard-blown snow, glare ice on lakes, puddles and creeks, or deep blankets of

soft snow after a sudden storm. Soft snow might cover low obstacles, making it impossible to judge exactly where to place the hoofs when running. Consequently, the hoofs are exposed to severe stresses, in particular if they fail to land squarely on level ground. Pronghorns have large, well-padded hoofs that separate widely. The front hoofs are larger than the rear hoofs and apparently absorb the high shocks of impact. Protruding dew claws could be damaged when running over rocky ground, in particular when

such is covered by snow. In flight, pronghorns attempt to keep a good sight line on danger, which leads pronghorns to elevated locations. That is, pronghorns in danger tend to head for high country.

The more one looks at a pronghorn, the more "design" features become evident that support high-speed running. The wind pipe of the pronghorn, the trachea, can be 5 inches in circumference and have a diameter exceeding 1½ inches, which is twice the diameter of a human trachea,

PRONGHORNS CAN DETECT and respond to an enemy at great distances. Science has not yet measured the pronghorn's vision, but field experiences suggest superlative eyesight.

though humans weigh twice as much as pronghorns. Thus the pronghorn's windpipe can move air about 4½ times the rate of the human windpipe. The pronghorn's skeleton is remarkably light, but the bone is very strong. Its skin is very thin, and it has much less body fat than does a deer. The pronghorn, which matches a domestic

North America had a species-rich *G J G*
assemblage of large, ofter

ANTIC

gigantic herbivores and carnivores

sheep in size, has a rumen much smaller than that of a sheep. Consequently, the pronghorn carries internally relatively little bone, fat, food and gut filling. This speaks to reducing excess baggage. That is, pronghorns travel light.

However, the pronghorn's heart is very large, twice the size of a sheep's heart. It has a big chest for large lungs and an advanced brain-cooling system. Running liberates a lot of metabolic heat, which can be dangerous on a hot summer day. The pronghorn's scapula is large and, in some individuals, it might have two well-formed parallel ridges, resembling the scapula of the extinct, long-legged bull-dog bear that it once shared the prairies with. The large muscles and muscle patterns around the scapula suggest the front legs can be quickly rotated to vary the hoof placement. The pronghorn's rostrum is remarkably large. This suggests its function is to adequately moisten and warm inspired air, in particular during winter cold snaps. After all, pronghorns must be prepared to run full tilt even in Arctic air. Cold, dry Arctic air is very damaging to lungs, which we know from medical research.

Which predators of the past shaped the pronghorn? Up until about 12,500 years ago, North America had an intact native big-game fauna that had developed over the previous 2 million years of the ice ages. This was a species-rich assemblage of large, often

BISON AND PRONGHORNS, back from the brink, in Custer State Park in South Dakota.

gigantic, herbivores and carnivores. Huge, long-legged Colombian mammoths, much larger than woolly mammoths, moved over the prairies. Long-tusked mastodons, as tall as Indian elephants but much more massive, roamed in the spruce forests. There were several species of horses, camels and ground sloths. The smallest ground sloths were the size of a grizzly bear. The largest sloths were the size of an elephant. There was a large-antlered moose with peculiarly twisted palms; a big, long-legged musk oxen; an enormous, long-horned bison; and a big mountain deer built like a mountain goat. There were also black-tailed and white-tailed deer. There were three species of peccaries, two of which grew as large as Russian wild boars. There were bighorn sheep and mountain goats as well as a giant "super-bighorn," a Eucerathere. The Eucerathere was the size of a modern bison, a distant relative of musk oxen, and it carried enormous curled horns.

The pronghorn was not without close relatives: A smaller four-horned rock-hopping pronghorn lived in the mountains, and a tiny, dainty four-horned species, little larger than a big jackrabbit, lived in the plains.

All these native herbivores show exceptional anti-predator specialization, quite understandable in view of the number and diversity of predators they lived with. There was a huge, carnivorous, short-faced bear, much larger and long-legged than Alaska brown or polar bears. It is also called the bull-dog bear. He must have sprinted hard after big bison and horses, bit hard

with powerful jaws, braced his big body and wrestled them quickly to the ground.

There were also two smaller species of short-faced bears. One lived on vegetable foods, and the other was a forest bear that lived with the smaller black bear. There was a lion, the same species as in Africa, but much, much larger. There were large prides of powerful, probably very noisy, saber-tooth tigers, which were the size of African lions. They specialized in quickly tearing down young mammoths and ground sloths with their powerful paws, and inflicting deep, lacerating bites to the abdomen — the one place their long, fragile sabers would not shatter on bone. Another cat, probably even more adept at spilling the guts of its prey, was the long-legged scimitar cat. It must have been a lone hunter capable of great speed, which ran up to the flanks of bison, horses or elephants, and with a quick, precise bite, cut long holes into the thin abdominal walls. That would spill the guts and tangle the legs of its victim in its own intestines. This cat, as large as a lion, had thin, broad, blade-like upper canines, just long enough for quick cutting through soft belly skins and tissues.

There was a cheetah-like running cat, but much bigger than today's African cheetah and probably just as fast — or faster. This, we suspect, was the pronghorn's foremost predator. There were also lynx, bobcats, big jaguars and mountain lions. There were packs of dire wolves, as large as Canadian gray wolves, but much more powerfully built, with larger heads and jaws. There were coyotes, though larger than today's coyotes, and there were red wolves.

ELK AND PRONGHORN mix on winter range in northern Yellowstone National Park.

There is sound reason for the pronghorn to look to the skies

Overhead, alongside the eagles, condors and hawks that survived, there sailed at least another dozen species of specialized raptors. Some of these were very large birds and probably of concern to pronghorns, just as golden eagles are today. These birds prey even on adults, not just young pronghorns. There was and still is sound reason for the pronghorn's eye to move up and down in a vertical plane and keep looking at the skies!

Only where there is a high diversity of specialized predators does it make sense to correctly identify the type of

A FENCE TRAPPED a fawn along a major highway in Wyoming, making it an easy meal for a mature bald eagle. Although the bald eagle is a common scavenger, his slightly smaller cousin, the golden eagle, is a skilled hunter of pronghorns. A carcass scavenged by birds remains intact, below. Coyotes and wolves dismember, crush and scatter bones.

predator before fleeing. With many species of predators about, it does not pay to run on suspicion, but only on certainty. Consequently, the pronghorn looks before it runs. This requires not only a superior eye, but also a superior brain to decipher the multitude of suspicious objects. There might not have been much point running from the stocky, slow saber-tooth tiger, but there might have been good reason to flee the similar, but long-legged scimitar cat. A crouching dire wolf might not have been a great danger, but a crouched American cheetah would have been. Given the sheer diversity of predators on the ice age prairies of unglaciated North America, it would have been a waste of resources to spook into costly running with every hint of a distant predator. Energy had to be conserved to use in body restoration, growth and reproduction. It was vital to identify predators precisely, and flee only from those that posed potential danger. Consequently, pronghorns had to be able to see as well as distinguish harmless from harmful predators in a timely manner. Yes, pronghorns had to be not only fleet of foot, but very smart!

All these American carnivores show significant specializations, while the American herbivores show extreme anti-predator adaptations. Evidently, in North America, but not in the Old World, there had been a very intense evolutionary race between carnivores

and herbivores. However, the teeth and feeding organs of the American herbivores remain remarkably primitive when compared to the refinements in feeding organs of comparable Eurasian forms. This indicates that herbivores in North America never got into severe food competition. It suggests the abundance and distribution of herbivores in North America was closely controlled by carnivores and not by the abundance of food, as was the case, apparently, in Eurasia. There is a less academic way of putting it: North America was then a predator hellhole!

Close examination of the bones of extinct North American predators reveals an unbelievable amount of damage, compared to the bones of comparable African forms today. Specialization by itself speaks of severe strain by predators trying to catch prey, just as sophisticated anti-predator adaptations of herbivores speak of severe demands on their bodies to escape being caught and eaten. The bones of extinct American carnivores, however, show so many healed fractures on the leg bones and paws, on the skull, on the backbone and ribs, that it becomes evident they worked very hard and took many risks to just eat. Once they caught up to their prey, flailing hoofs, horns, tusks and claws extracted a heavy toll from these predators. Many of their prey species were big-bodied and must have been very nasty opponents. No doubt, being a predator — or a prey species — in North America during the ice ages was a very hard fate.

The results of this merciless, unceasing competition between American predators and prey is manifest to this day. The surviving old North American species — such as coyote, peccary, pronghorn, black bear, mountain lion and white-tailed or black-tailed deer — are extremely good at avoiding man-made trouble. They are very smart. They must be in order to live in close proximity to people and — normally — go undetected. No roe deer or wild boar from Europe can do this, but our deer and peccaries do. However, as expected, where they have met comparable Old World species, as did white-tailed and black-tailed deer released in Europe or New Zealand, the old Americans turned out to be poor competitors. Even against Asiatic sika deer introduced to native white-tailed deer range, our whitetails are no match.

Yet as survival artists in the face of human prosecution, native North American ice-age species know no peer.

For example, gray wolves and grizzly bears — which came along with man only 10,000 to 12,000 years ago from Eastern Siberia to lower North America — were targeted for destruction early this century by Western stock growers in the United States. They were quickly eliminated. Stock growers also targeted the coyote, but they did not eliminate this smart fellow. Studies of radio-collared wolves reveal — at times — a pathetic, rock-stupid animal. No one can make such accusations about coyotes, black bears or mountain lions, or even white-tailed deer.

When you see a

SALUTE

pronghorn on the prairie, salute the lively, little fellow

These are thriving. Coyotes and deer are dramatically expanding their range. Black bears can coexist with humans to a remarkable degree, even in suburbs, as can white-tailed or black-tailed deer, even pronghorns and mountain lions — to say nothing of coyotes. There might be shortages of wolves and grizzly bears, but who has heard recently of shortages of coyotes, black bears, pumas or white-tailed deer? Who has ever heard of wolves and grizzly bears thriving in city parks? Who has ever asked for coyotes to be returned at great public expense and political controversy to some ecosystem they happen to be missing from?

The native American predators of the ice ages were diverse, specialized and hard driving, but the pronghorn bested them all. This is significant, because even we humans did not. It now appears these large predators kept man from entering North America for tens of thousands of years. As long as America's gigantic predators and prey species were alive and well, humans failed to even get a toe hold in North America, let alone settle or thrive. Modern humans colonized all continents, except Antarctica, almost 40,000 years ago, even crossing ocean gaps as wide as 70 miles. But they failed in North America. Yet humans did reach South America then, which archaeological evidence increasingly indicates. However, they might not have prospered there. In North America, humans only show up with the beginning of megafaunal extinction, namely after the huge carnivorous bull-dog bear went extinct.

That happened during a severe cold spell that suddenly interrupted the last deglaciation about 12,500 years ago. The American cheetah died out along with the bull-dog bear. Then, for a millennium, the numbers of elephants, horses, camels, bison, etc., rose to very high levels. It was as if the large prey species rebounded from severe predation pressure. Then humans made their appearance and, within less than 500 years, exterminated the Colombian mammoth. Human numbers rose slowly over the next 6,000 years, in step with the extinction of the rich North American native big-game fauna. It is as if America's native large mammals were a brake on human colonization and expansion.

Other Siberian big-game species moved with man to occupy the ecological vacuum left by the extinction of North America's native species, Siberians such as elk, bison, moose, grizzly bear, gray wolf and wolverine. An impoverished new fauna of Siberian immigrants and old American survivors formed on the continent, poorly adapted to one another, and the Siberians poorly adapted to the landscape as well. A brand new faunal history was about to commence here, till, of course Europeans arrived and put it all in jeopardy.

When you next see a pronghorn on the prairie, salute the lively little fellow. It braved predators even we could not master, and come through hell to enrich our lives.

This is one tough, smart American.

PRAIRIE DOGS DIG HOLES that flip horses and cows, but not pronghorns. Although a prairie dog town is a potential trap for unwary legs, it also creates habitat for pronghorns.

CHAPTER 3

ITS PLACE IN THE ANIMAL KINGDOM

Few species have generated more debate about their place in the order of life than the pronghorn. It is a bundle of oddities. In fact, the more we get to know about the pronghorn, the foggier things become.

Is it an antelope? Is it a goat? Is it a deer? Is it a bear? Few species have generated more debate about their place in the order of life than the pronghorn. The pronghorn and its family were confined entirely to North America. On one hand, it shares striking behavioral features with the African and Asian gazelles and dwarf antelope. On the other, it shares diverse features with the Siberian roe deer. The pronghorn's legs resemble those of the giraffe. The horns of pronghorn bucks are forked, the only forked horns we know of. The horns are positioned on horn cores rising from the upper rim of the orbit, an ancient characteristic not found in true antelopes or in deer. Moreover, the horn core is covered with fairly dense, long white hair.

Nothing comparable is found in bovids. The horns are shed annually, and regrow from the tip of the horn core, spreading horn mass up as well as down. This, too, is unique. Judge Caton reported that horn shedding was first described in a manuscript sent by Dr. C.A. Canfield of Monterey, Calif., on April 10, 1828, to the Smithsonian Institution for publication. The incredulous editor, Professor Baird, held it back for confirmation, and finally published the paper in February 1835, almost seven years after receiving it. That delay might still stand as a record of sort.

Note, the horns do not peel or splinter off under the stresses and strains of use, but as we shall see later, are shed and regrown in an orderly fashion in a perfectly meaningful, harmonious context within the

Despite their striking coloration, resting pronghorns melt into the ground, becoming all but invisible. Males might stick out because of their black faces and horns. When the horns are only ear-length, even mature bucks might be difficult to distinguish from females at a distance.

The horns are shed and regrow
in a perfectly meaningful, ha

OUS

nonious context

pronghorn's biology. The accidental exfoliation of horns in some bovids cannot be compared to horn shedding in pronghorn bucks. Scientists always promise that more research will clarify matters. It's a reflex with them! However, it seems the more we get to know about the pronghorn, the foggier things become. The latest puzzle is that some pronghorn shoulder blades have two parallel ridges, resembling closely the shoulder blade of the extinct, high-speed bull-dog bear of North America's Ice Age prairies. That does not make the pronghorn a bear, though it is a bundle of oddities! Let us begin with matters not contentious.

The pronghorn is a small ruminant, or cud chewer. That stands for an old, efficient way to digest cellulose and hemi-cellulose using bacterial fermentation. Fermentation takes place in the large rumen, ahead of the true stomach, and again in an intestinal sac at the end of the small intestines called a caecum. Most of the energy fermented out of the plant food is absorbed directly into the blood stream from the respective fermentation vats. The rumen, along with the liver and kidney, also functions to detoxify the many plant poisons ingested by pronghorns. Because the pronghorn selects plant parts high in nutrients and energy, its rumen is rather small. We call pronghorns "concentrate feeders," a similarity pronghorns share with white-tailed deer. Because the most nutritious parts of plants tend to be protected by poisons, the pronghorn developed into a detoxification specialist.

On Northern ranges, pronghorn bucks weigh

RIGHT AFTER THE RUT, bucks shed their old horns. Few shed both at once. On the tip of the dark-skinned horn core, clad in white hair, sits the bud of the new horn. A close-up look at a shed horn, above, reveals the embedded white hairs. The keratin, which forms the bulk of the horn, flows around and engulfs the hairs at the horn core.

about 121 pounds and females about 110 pounds. The buck's weight advantage is only 10 percent or 1.1, which is typical of many plains-dwelling ruminants. Bucks are heavier by about 17.6 pounds at the end of summer before the rut, than in November after the rut. The does fluctuate less in weight than the bucks. Pronghorns thus gain and lose less body fat seasonally than deer, elk or moose. The buck stands about 35 inches at the shoulder, and the doe almost an inch less.

On Southern ranges, in the deserts of Mexico and Arizona, pronghorn bucks weigh about 88 pounds and does about 80 pounds. As a rule, members of a species increase in body mass latitudinally up to the 60th parallel north, and – contrary to Bergmann's Rule – rapidly decrease in mass thereafter. That is, they get bigger from south to north and decrease in size north of 60 degrees latitude. Pronghorn distribution falls well short of the 60th parallel, so they can only increase in size south to north, with lots of exceptions in between. We expect pronghorns to vary in body size with the number of contiguous days of good feeding available to fawns. This can be short in deserts, resulting in small bodies. By and large, pronghorns do best where there is adequate water and the vegetation is not excessively dry.

Pronghorn do not do well in deserts

Thus, they do not do well in deserts, and suffer severe mortality during droughts. As one would expect, they might do very well and grow large bodies, where they have access to irrigated crops and hayfields. Very large pronghorns are found on high elevation ranges in California, southwestern Oregon and northern Nevada. Elevation does compensate for latitude.

Compared to the size of its extinct relatives of the recent Ice Age, the pronghorn is big. A mature buck of the extinct four-horned Conclin's pronghorn (*Stockoceros*) of the Southwest must have weighed about 77 pounds. Along with a relatively larger set of horns than our pronghorn, the Conclin's had relatively shorter, stockier legs. It might have lived in shrubby, hilly terrain and was probably a saltor, that is, adapted to running with big jumps. The other long-surviving relative of the pronghorn, but now extinct, was the tiny *Capromeryx minor*. A big one would have weighed 22 pounds and stood 22 inches at the shoulder. This delicate little four-horned pronghorn resembled some of the African dwarf antelope. It was apparently a plains dweller that went extinct about 10,000 years ago, along with so many American big-game species. Several earlier species of pronghorn had up to six horn cores, and some even had twisted horn cores, not unlike kudu antelope of Africa. Even so, none exceeded the current pronghorn noticeably in size. Antilocaprids were historically small ruminants.

The horns of pronghorns are unusual in that each horn has a prong, the horns are shed in a regular

WATER IS NOT A LUXURY to pronghorns, but it is essential for superior growth and reproduction. Plant communities near water bodies are inevitably richer in high-quality feed.

The horn cores bear
a remarkable similarity to the ears

fashion annually, they are attached to the horn core in an unusual fashion, and they grow from the tip of the horn core, both up and down. When the buck's horns are shed in late October or early November, the horn cores are covered with long, whitish hair. Horn cores are about as long as the ears and bear a remarkable similarity to them. It is as if horn cores mimic ears, and by so doing allow the buck to integrate into the large female herds in late fall and winter. I once wrote an opinion to this effect to a judge on behalf of a hunter who accidentally shot a buck that had shed its horns. The hunter had a female tag and claimed he had mistaken the buck for a female. The game warden suspected the hunter had shot a horned buck, removed the horn sheaths, and then played innocent.

Yet, adult pronghorn are remarkably similar in color, and one can easily confuse males and females, especially after the bucks shed their horns. Still, the sexes have their differences. The buck has a dark nose and rostrum, a mask, and a large black patch below the ear. This black patch contains an actively

secreting gland that produces a pungent odor. The buck uses this gland to mark protruding vegetation on his territory. Bucks might be difficult to distinguish from females, but they can always be picked out by their dark face mask and dark cheek patch. These are permanent, and are even recognizable in fawns when they assume the adult coat.

The horns are true horn, but they also have incorporated a large amount of hair within the horn substance, which holds the horn firmly to the horn core. The new horn grows from the tip of the horn core, and probably pushes the old horn off the horn core, tearing the imbedded hairs out of the core's skin. At shedding, the little horn on top of each core is quite soft except for the tip, which is also light in color. Except for the tip, the horn mass is dark and remains so while growing. It grows rapidly up as well as down from the tip. In growing downward, the soft horn mass engulfs the fuzzy white hair. At the growing sites, the skin of the horn core is thick, well-perfused with blood, and warm to the touch.

The horn's curved upper portion is grown normally from late October to late January. It then grows the characteristic fork. It starts off low on the horn core, but is pushed upward as the horn growth continues. All the while, the horn core's long white hair is incorporated into the horn mass. This gives the horn's exterior the typical fibrous, longitudinally

THE BUD OF THE NEW HORN is soft, warm, rubbery and white-tipped. However, it will soon grow hard and sharp. During the winter, it extends downward and upward into a black horn, as well as laterally, forming a fork.

furrowed, rough texture. When fork growth commences in February, there might be a brief burst of horn growth in all directions, resulting occasionally in randomly protruding tiny horn-points, or burrs. The horn grows right into July. The buck's horns are fully grown and unblemished between July and September when the rutting season begins, and the horn sheaths might suffer damage in fighting. Casting usually occurs about a week after the mating season, between Oct. 15 and Nov. 15. By January, older bucks might have grown as much as 3 inches of new horn, though none has as yet a fork. The forks appear earlier in old bucks. These might not grow the fork till May. In the meantime, the shed horn sheaths soon disintegrate. Rodents and coyotes often nibble and chew the shed horns.

The shape of the horns allows bucks to lock their heads in powerful wrestling contests. The horn curves inward at the tip, which normally prevents injury during sparring, for a horn thrust directed against the body usually causes skin punctures. Wounding, however, might occur in serious fights as horns vigorously twist, with horn tips piercing and tearing an opponent's neck. The prongs normally prevent an opponent's horns from sliding past. Thus, combatants frequently lock heads at the level of the prongs. However, they might slip further and then fight head-to-head. The pronghorn's horn structure is, in principle, similar to that of other species that spend virtually all their life in the com-

LOOK CLOSELY. Bucks and does differ in head markings. Does do not have the black gland patch below the ear, and their nose tip is black. Females might have horns, but only small ones. Bucks have thicker necks.

pany of others in large herds. Such grouping is an anti-predator adaptation, and is labeled "the selfish herd." In such a grouping, it's vital not to wound, because blood and festering wounds attract predators. If a buck wounds a companion in the herd, it endangers its own life indirectly. Consequently, natural selection rapidly selects for a horn shape that, in normal use, allows wrestling but not wounding.

A horn shape that fosters wrestling leads to another significant development in pronghorns: The bucks can use their weapons in harmless "sporting engagements," which we call sparring. In the complex world of antlered deer and antelope, this is a way to form bonds among males. Thus, pronghorn bucks appear to enjoy tussles as much as we enjoy sport. It opens a dimension in their social life that is foreclosed to species that defend resource territories and whose weapons are used primarily to inflict wounds, as exemplified, for instance, by the mountain goat.

Female pronghorns may have short unbranched horns, which they also shed and regrow, but irregu-

COYOTES AND RODENTS chew shed antelope horns. Intact horn sheaths soon weather, and might look deceptively like old branches of sage.

larly. By January, some does can have up to an inch of horns. Bart O'Gara reports that several years' worth of horn cones may stick together in some females, and that female horns can be lifted off easily in some individuals at all seasons. The horn-growth cycle of females is, therefore, not regular. Kids might also grow hornlets, which they might shed already in January. In females, the horns may not be noticeable till they are yearlings. In male kids, however, horns may be felt early under the skin. In poorly grown kids, horns may not be shed till spring.

The short spiky horns in females suggest that these are used occasionally to defend something against other pronghorns with short horns. Horns in females are not uncommon in plains-dwelling species of antelope and deer that live in herds. The horns of females usually match in size those of young males. Observations suggest that females use them to keep young males in check. In pronghorns, this matter needs examining, but I'm betting young bucks will try to displace females from craters that females paw in snow to reach food buried beneath. Horns do not ensure elevated social rank in pronghorn does, nor are they regularly employed against coyotes. Rather, female pronghorns attacking coyotes do so usually with their front legs.

Not only the horns are unusual in pronghorns. So is their placement on the head. The pronghorn is the only surviving species in which the horn cores grow from the upper rim of the orbits. In bovids and cervids, horn-like organs grow from the frontal bones. This is a primitive, ancient condition.

The hair coat is composed of thick, tough, yet brittle hairs with large air cells. The undercoating is sparse by comparison and composed of fine hair. The pigmented guard hairs are 1½ to 2 inches long, and the erectile white hairs of the rump patch are up to 3 inches long. The pronghorn can erect hair on the rump patch into a large, disk-shaped rosette. This is one characteristic it shares with the Eurasian roe deer. As in roe deer, the pronghorn's tail is very short, almost inconspicuous. In addition, pronghorns have glands in the rump patches that appear to release scent when they're aroused. This might leave enough scent suspended in the air for fawns to follow running mothers at night. Another gland, the median, is located on the back ahead of the rump patch. During displays, bucks raise the hair around the gland.

The hair coat is very light compared to its bulk,

and gives adequate protection even during Arctic cold spells when temperatures descend below -40 degrees Fahrenheit. During blizzards, pronghorns hunker down on the ground, facing away from the wind and blowing snow. They are remarkably tolerant of cold and high wind. The hairs are readily raised and lowered, which suggests the body surface might be quickly ventilated as need be. This is vital in a fast runner, because fast running generates a large amount of internal body heat. This heat must be shed quickly, even on boiling hot summer days in Southern deserts where daytime

AFTER THE RUT, but before shedding their horns, bucks begin to re-establish bonds, right, as witnessed by grossly unequal sparring matches. During the rut, below, not all horn contact leads to severe fighting. Territorial neighbors might reinforce positions by a brief sparring match.

temperatures reach 105 degrees Fahrenheit. Thus, the hair coat must be able to conserve heat during severe cold, but also shed body heat as soon as required. The hair sheds starting in March, and the new coat grows in by mid-June. Pronghorns do not have a distinct summer coat, as do mule and white-tailed deer. Consequently, they have only one hair change each year.

A pronounced feature of this coat is not only the erectile hair on the caudal disk, but also the erectile hair on the back of the neck. This hair is fringed in black, so the neckline is much pronounced and the neck much enlarged when a displaying pronghorn raises its hair. These dorsal neck hairs might be 3 to 4 inches long. They're erected by both sexes, but especially the bucks, beginning at an early age. They're a vital part of the social signals.

Pronghorns feed on a large number of browse, forbs, grass and sedge species. The dominant food species throughout the year on Northern range are various species of sage (*Artemesia*). In winter, collectively, these might make up to 80 percent of the rumen content. This is remarkable, because the essential oils of sage brush are known to be toxic and to inhibit rumen function in other ruminants. Yet a predominance of toxic plants characterize the food habits of pronghorns.

LIFE IN THE HERD has its rewards. With the rut and horn shedding behind them, bucks turn to a friendly sparring match, a playful, relaxed social activity that bonds bucks — even if one mounts the other in a dominance display.

They even feed on plants deadly to livestock, such as loco weed, grease wood, rabbit bush, lark spur, broom weed, silvery lupine, leaf spurgen and arrow-leafed milk vetch. It appears that pronghorns have specialized in feeding on highly nutritious vegetation that is normally protected against being eaten by high levels of toxic chemicals. Sagebrush is no exception, because it contains high levels of protein, fat and carbohydrates. However, in Southern deserts, even pronghorns may have difficulties with some toxic plants, particularly if they're already malnourished.

Consider: Domestic sheep, which are about as large as pronghorns, are grazers. They take in large amounts of rather fibrous, nontoxic grasses that are difficult and slow to digest. Pronghorns, by contrast, take in less per day, but more nutritious food that is protected by plant toxins. Pronghorns have rumens – primary fermentation chambers – that are less than half as large as those of sheep, and a caecum – secondary fermentation chamber – that is less than two-thirds as large. They consume about 3½ pounds of dry plant food per day compared to 7 pounds for sheep. However, the pronghorn's liver, one of the organs responsible for detoxifying plant compounds, is about twice as large as a sheep's. The pronghorn's kidneys are also larger than a sheep's. Here are two different feeding strategies: The pronghorn is classified as a "concentrate feeder." Nevertheless, a small overlap in food habits exists between pronghorns and domestic sheep. The sheep get the better of pronghorns on depleted ranges, because pronghorns depend more on succulent forbs than do sheep. The

Antelope have a way to form
friendships among males

overlap in food habits between cattle and prong-horns is small, as is the overlap between bison and pronghorns.

Food habits vary regionally, which should be expected, given the pronghorn's wide geographic distribution. Still, shrubs and various dicotyledonous plants predominate, although freshly sprouting grasses might be avidly consumed, particularly in spring and again after a summer's drought when autumnal rains stimulate grass growth. During wet years in its Southern distribution, pronghorns primarily eat succulent forbs. During drought years, they primarily use browse species. Nor are agricultural crops shunned by pronghorns, such as alfalfa and winter wheat. The latter can become an important winter food in Northern prairie regions. Here, pronghorns avidly eat the first flush of green grasses in spring. This food source will be supplanted by succulent forbs as these begin to sprout. In summer and early fall, pronghorns feed on a variety of plants. In winter, it might be primarily sage brush and junipers. In Southern deserts, the diminutive prong-horns feed on bursage, mesquite, chain fruit cholla (a cactus), mistletoe, iron wood, palo verde, and even ceosote bush. During rainy years they feed on succulent forbs growing on alluvial flats, where water quickly runs off, unable to penetrate the hard pan. Two rainy seasons affect plant growth here; the "monsoon" rains between July and September, and the winter rains from December through February. The washes might hold flowing water briefly during the monsoons.

Although pronghorns are not grazers, they have a dentition typical of advanced grazers. These animals notoriously evolve long, ever-growing cheek teeth to

counter the abrasion of grasses on teeth. In prong-horns, abrasion is not caused by the silicatious crystals inside the grasses, but by the dust and grit blown about on the prairie and deposited on vegetation. The prairie can be a dusty place to live, particularly during severe droughts. Dust may blow about then as "black blizzards." During glaciations, continental glaciers grind rock into fine powder, which is born by water as silt. When silt dries after floods recede, the rock dust is blown about by winds and redeposited as loess. The bigger the glaciers, the more

dust. So dusty was the air of the past glacial periods that dust was deposited in annual layers on the glaciers of Greenland, as revealed by cores drilled in its ice cap. Abrasive dust has been the pronghorn's faithful companion.

Prairie fires do a lot of good for pronghorns. They may singe off the spines of cactus lobes and when that happens, pronghorns descend from near and far for a feast. Cacti are nutritious, but are, of course, well-protected by their nasty thorns against being eaten. Prairie fires might also remove dense mats of

THE LONG HAIR of the rump patch, when erected, is visible at long distances as an alarm response.

roses and snowberry scrub, which are followed by an abundance of forbs the following spring. Vegetation on burns tends to erupt earlier in the year, as the dark, exposed ground heats up faster under the rays of the spring sun. Thus, burns allow pronghorns to feed on the nutritionally superior sprouting forage earlier in the year, and switch to sprouting forage when it finally erupts on unburned prairie. This increases the number of days pronghorns can feed on superior food. However, the positive effects of fire on vegetation pass quickly in grasslands. By the second summer, the burn is no longer conspicuously favored by pronghorns. In the shrub steppe, the positive effect of fires might last many more years.

Pronghorns also take advantage of riparian, that is, waterline vegetation. In the Northern and Central prairies, the melt-off of snow packs fill many shallow depressions with water. These sloughs might dry out in summer. As they dry, their wet fringes are filled by various pioneering weeds and grasses. A particular favorite of pronghorns is sour dock. In their Southern distribution, water courses – permanent or otherwise – might provide rich feed when the waters recede. In the South, pronghorns might do well and grow very large in body and horns when living near permanent streams with native grasslands fanning back from the water. In deserts, pronghorns might be attracted to sand dunes, just like camels in the Sahara. Sand dunes tend to store water and thus enhance the growth of vegetation, particu-

When water bodies formed by melting snow and rain shrink, a green rim of sprouting vegetation follows the water's edge. Such vegetation is nutritious and avidly sought by pronghorns.

larly annual forbs, which erupt briefly in spring before desiccating in the summer heat.

While pronghorns do noticeably better where and when water is reasonably abundant, they drink little if vegetation is succulent. Once the food's water content declines below 75 percent, pronghorns are more likely to drink from open water. Their maximum water intake is about 7 pints.

Pronghorns normally give birth to large twins, which grow up rapidly, mature early, become adults soon – and die young. Life is fast-paced for pronghorns. Twins in Northern localities average nearly 8½ pounds at birth, which is large compared to newborns of other terrestrial mammals as large as pronghorns. Thus, the maternal investment in young is very high, not uncommon in plains-dwelling ruminants. The gestation period of 250 days is long for so small a ruminant, but that has a good reason, which I shall detail later. In the North, the fawning season is short, lasting about three weeks, but it is extended in the Southern deserts. Pronghorns time their births to fall just ahead of the period of maximum productivity of green, succulent plants. That ensures a rich food supply for females, which must produce a maximum of milk for the fawns.

Twins grow rapidly on the nutrient-rich milk of their mother. At 25 percent, the milk solids in pronghorn milk are twice as high as those in the milk of domestic cattle. Pronghorn milk at 13 percent fat is remarkably rich. Pronghorn fawns must rapidly grow to "survivable" – that is, adult size – and do so virtually in six

months. This is typical of plains dwellers closely cropped by wolves or cheetah-like carnivores that run down their prey. Fawn production and survival are highly variable regionally. Reproduction is highest when females can feed prenatally and post-natally on abundant succulent forbs through the lactation period. Droughts, overgrazed ranges and life in deserts can lead to small fawns, small fawn crops, poor fawn survival, late maturation and small adults.

Fawns are classical hiders at birth. They separate and lie down close to objects that break their outline when viewed from above. Except for the long gestation period, the pronghorn's overall reproductive biology resembles that of the saiga antelope from Russia and Mongolia, which is also a small, highly gregarious, cursorial plains ruminant that lives on abrasive, dust-covered forbs.

Pronghorns vary little regionally. The species has been traditionally carved into five subspecies: the American pronghorn, *Antilocapra americana americana Ord* 1818; the Oregon pronghorn, *A. a. oregona Bailey* 1932; the Mexican pronghorn, *A. a. mexicana Merriam* 1901; Peninsular pronghorn from Baja California, *A. a. peninsularis Nelson* 1912; and

AN ENORMOUS WILDFIRE spewing smoke leads to a spectacular sunset. Fires are a friend of pronghorns. Prairie fires burn away vegetation unfavorable to pronghorns and replace it, for a few years, with nutritious, high-quality plants.

FIRES
Prairie fires do a lot of good for pronghorns

The fawns are classic hiders at birth

Sonoran pronghorn from northern Mexico, *A. a. sonoriensis Goldman* 1945. Now, all that looks terribly officious and pompously scientific. However, it is almost certainly of little significance. Having had ample time and incentive to pursue the matter of official subspecies, and testify about such in courts of law as an expert witness, I noticed with some dismay that no descriptions of pronghorn subspecies tried to differentiate between environmental adjustment and genetic adaptation. Nor did they give an adequate description, let alone analysis, of natural population variations. Although the slight regional differences might be valid and of taxonomic significance, it hasn't been proven. Nor has it been determined whether the differences are ecotypic or taxonomic, that is, whether they are the product of different environments on similar genotypes or the expression of different hereditary factors.

Moreover, body size differences between regions are so trivial as to be likely environmental in origin. With that, the greatest difference would vanish. "Sonoran pronghorn" are likely seasonally undernourished pronghorns that would grow to large size under good forage conditions. Any significant recovery of these would lead to big-bodied pronghorns as exist already in Arizona, New Mexico and Texas where forage conditions are good. What has been purported as diagnostic features appear to be differences based on small sample size and thus statistically out of context. I am fairly confident the traditional pronghorn taxonomy will not survive court scrutiny, which is likely to happen sooner than later as formal taxonomic names now have legal standing in conservation legislation and are actionable in court. It is high time that pronghorn taxonomy be based on acceptable, let alone, good science.

So far, the foregoing has shed precious little light on the pronghorn's origin and classification. Its characteristics are virtually all answers to ecological problems of ice ages past. Its

THIS PREGNANT PRONGHORN doe, left, bloated with young, will feed on green, late-spring range. The births are timed to coincide with nutritious forage. Below, fawns might camouflage themselves from aerial predators by lying close to spots of bare soil and animal droppings to break their outlines.

security adaptations are unique and do not shed light on pronghorn origins. Nor does anything in the above. So what about its fossil history?

Pronghorns arose in North America. Their distant ancestors apparently came from Asia about 20 million years ago during the Tertiary Period, the so called Age of Mammals. Pronghorns arose in the Pliocene. Their predecessors, the Mericoidontidae, were as fantastic a group of creatures as ever walked the Earth. They were plains-dwelling ruminants, rather small and dainty with very odd "antler-horns." Despite determined attempts, they have defied deciphering. However, the "horns" of mericoidontids are so odd as to be outside anything we know. They are antler-like in that they freely branch like antlers. However, they were not shed. Were they branching horn cores?

They had some sort of covering. Moreover, that covering appears to have been shed. Bone rings surround the base of the "antlers." These have been interpreted as remnants of a cover that was shed. Clearly, the mericoidontids took their secrets to the grave. If these creatures were the ancestors of pronghorns, then whatever similarities pronghorns have to true bovids are because of convergent evolution. That would mean that taxonomically, pronghorns are simply pronghorns. It is a uniquely American ruminant, and worthy of a family of its own, the *Antilocapridae*. They are not antelopes, goats, deer or giraffes, of sort. They are pronghorns, nothing more and nothing less.

FAWNS ARE SOON lively replicas of their parents. These fawns are large enough to outrun coyotes.

CHAPTER 4

PLAYING THE MATING GAME

Territory is an important adaptive strategy for the pronghorn. Bucks develop defended spaces and guard their does. Establishing these areas involves much bravado as females seek out a confident buck in this courtship process.

You may have noticed in the preceding chapters that discussing each feature of pronghorns in isolation did not shed much light on them. However, a cluster of features held together logically by a common theme did generate explanations. One such theme is that pronghorns are runners, severely tested by now extinct carnivores. A theme can also be labeled an "adaptive syndrome or strategy." Within each theme, some of the features characterizing pronghorns are logically related to an adaptive function. Thus, starting with the pronghorn's exceptionally large eyes, one could relate them to the specialized legs and shoulder blades, the large heart, the small rumen and caecum, the low fat content of the body, the very light skin and hair, the large trachea and rostrum — all of which had a logical place within the security strategies of the pronghorn as a runner, which was adapted to spot and interpret distant signs of predators and to traverse uneven terrain at very high speeds, day or night.

There are other adaptive strategies that tie together — and thus explain — diverse features of the pronghorn. One of the most important is territoriality, a discovery we owe to Peter Bromley's early research on pronghorns in Montana. The pronghorn buck places a breeding territory, a defended space, over the best feeding sites of females and excludes it from other bucks.

A BUCK CUTTING OFF an escaping female. The buck is rounding up the doe and will try to return her to the center of his territory and harem.

In this, the pronghorn resembles the roe deer of Eurasia, which happens to have evolved much the same reproductive strategy. Here is an example of a highly specialized plains runner and a short-winded saltor and hider in thick forests — none related to the other — hitting upon the very same solution of how to reproduce in climates with long, cold winters while retaining a small body size.

Pronghorns were small historically. Why they failed to evolve large bodies as deer and bovids did remains a puzzle. We have to take their small size as a given, even though small size in a temperate climate confers liabilities. Thus pronghorns, like all ruminants from cold-temperate climates, be they large or small, have to give birth just as green-up takes place in late spring. That allows the female to feed on rich forage before birth, which fosters the growth of her babies and allows her to produce rich milk in abundance after birth. This helps the young grow rapidly. The larger the kids in fall, the more capable they are of dealing with hard winters and predators. However, gestation periods vary with body size — the larger the species, the longer the gestation period. Consequently, large-bodied species must rut early in the year to give birth in late spring, while small-bodied species must rut late in the year to achieve the same. For instance, to give birth to a calf in early June, moose, because they are so big, must rut in late September. Caribou, which are smaller than moose, rut in mid- to late October. White-tailed deer, because they are smaller still, mate in November to early December. Pronghorns, which are much smaller than white-tailed deer, by rightful expectation should rut in the first half of January. However, they do not. Pronghorns rut in late September. Consequently, they have a very long gestation period of about 250 days, matching that of the moose, which is eight to 10 times larger than the pronghorn.

Having a rutting season in January would be difficult for pronghorns. The bucks would need a heavy load of stored body fat to fuel the costly activities of fighting, running and guarding females, as well as healing battle wounds after the rut. Healing wounds is very costly! Yet accumulating a heavy load of fat would interfere with the pronghorn's speed and endurance. Pronghorns need to stay fairly lean to generate high, sustained speed. Fat pronghorns are expected to be vulnerable to wolves, just as fat caribou bulls are before the rut.

Nor could pronghorns pay for the costly rutting activities in January by increasing food intake. In January, forage is very limited, of fairly low quality, and might be periodically

inaccessible because of storms dumping snow on the land, which forces pronghorns to paw the snow away or move long distances beyond the storm's reach. Both alternatives are expensive in energy. So is the loss of body heat to windy days when cold Arctic air masses cover the prairie. As the wind-chill increases, pronghorns terminate feeding and hunker down facing away from the wind. In short, rutting activities would be interrupted by movements of females because of poor food, deep snow or severe wind chill. It is sensible to place the rutting season at a less constraining time.

The roe deer of Eurasia has evolved a similar reproductive strategy as the pronghorn, but has gone further in some adaptations. It is as small as the pronghorn in Siberia, but smaller-bodied in its southern distribution in Western China and in Europe. Also, it has backed its mating season by more than a month into August. In addition, it evolved delayed implantation. The egg fertilized by the roe buck in August quickly assumes the blastula stage, but does not

BUCKS SHOW TERRITORIAL behavior early in the year, such as this buck, below, herding pregnant does and yearlings at the end of May.

implant into the female's uterine wall till January. That is when roe deer, theoretically, ought to be rutting were it not for their small size. Thus roe deer have a gestation period of 276 to 295 days, longer still than that of pronghorns. Like pronghorns, roe deer are lean-bodied. In both species, the males become territorial in summer long before the mating season, and they

WHEN BUCKS BECOME TERRITORIAL, below, the defender is frequently called upon to chase off challengers. Bucks with their tongues hanging out are not an uncommon sight. Right, does are run hard by lesser male intruders into harems unprotected by dominant males.

shed their short antlers or horns shortly after the rut when the males join the large female herds. In both species, the males grow their antlers or horns during winter so their weaponry is ready to be used in spring or early summer. There are a few nontrivial differences: Roe bucks bond yearling females to their respective territories with sex that involves lengthy courtship and attention by the buck to a prospective female resident of his territory. Pronghorn bucks have a urination-defecation ceremony almost identical to that of gazelles. Roe deer mark by horning saplings with secretion of the frontal glands. In addition, the roe buck tears up ground and defecates where he

mating season

horned and pawed. Pronghorns mark vegetation selectively, just like gazelle, but with the subauricular glands below the ears rather than with the preorbital glands ahead of the eyes as found in gazelles. Subordinate bucks in roe deer and pronghorns are relegated to inferior habitat by the intolerance of dominant territorial bucks. There is thus a remarkable similarity between roe deer and pronghorn bucks.

Backing the rutting season into early fall or late summer accomplishes an important feat. The high cost of rutting can be born directly by late summer or early fall vegetation phenology. That alleviates the need for fattening in pronghorns

DURING THE RUT, the territorial buck withdraws with each estrous doe into a hiding place for undisturbed breeding. In his absence, lesser bucks invade the harem and might chase does severely. The female attempts to evade this harassment by urinating. The urine is attractive to males, and they pause to test it.

and roe bucks to pay for the high cost of rutting. Consequently, although both species store a little fat before rutting, they remain rather lean in fall compared to elk, deer or moose. It's more efficient not to fatten, because energy liberated by digestion can be used directly to pay the metabolic cost, instead of putting the energy through

G R E E N

Although the green-up provide
it does no

the very costly process of storing fat. We noted earlier that pronghorns store proportionately half the fat or less than elk, deer or moose.

Pronghorns use the early phase of plant growth in early summer, or green-up, to pay the high costs of late gestation and lactation, but also to grow a new hair coat, finish the final horn growth, and restore the depleted body after winter's hardships. Although green-up provides the best food, it does not pay for the rut. However, bucks do come into good body condition, which includes a slight marbling of their meat with fat. Roe bucks, by comparison fatten a little with green-up, and then use it all on establishing their territory. Then, they pause, refatten and use these stores to pay for courtship and fighting when the females come into heat. Thus roe bucks fatten — a little — twice before the rut.

Following the early phase of plant growth is a midsummer period when forage plants become rather fibrous, while browsed plants develop various toxins to discourage herbivores. Such mature vegetation is poor forage. However, it is followed by a wave of seed and fruit ripening, followed by early fall frosts killing herbaceous plants and turning the dead leaves into nutritious natural ensilage. This in turn is followed by snow, cold, low food availability and reduced forage quality. However, the period of seed and fruit ripening is a good time to feed on large amounts of highly digestible food. In addition, rains might restore some grass and herbal growth in early fall. It is this second pulse of good food

that pronghorns appear to exploit during the rut. Therefore, pronghorn bucks do not interfere with the gestating-lactating and recuperating females during the green-up, but rather use the second food pulse of late summer and early fall to pay for the high cost of rutting.

Pronghorns and roe deer have not only chosen an advanced time of year to mate, but take remarkably similar steps to make it happen. Bucks of large size and advanced age claim possession of a large area of very good habitat where females come to feed and raise their young, and exclude other bucks by force. Thus, territorial bucks and females are on prime habitat, while bachelors are relegated to poorer habitats. If high-quality forage is scarce, the exclusion of bachelor bucks from prime feeding sites might contribute to the females' ability to produce more milk and superior fawns. Success hinges not on bulk forage, but on preferential access to the rather small amounts of high quality, highly digestible forage that can be quickly creamed off. As small-bodied ruminants, pronghorns depend on the highest quality forage for success.

Territories are established well ahead of mating time. In pronghorns, this begins in late spring, well before the bucks have finished grow-

A PRONGHORN BUCK IN LATE SPRING during green-up shares his habitat with a cow elk, below. The buck, horns grown, is beginning to shed his well-worn winter coat.

the best food,
pay for the rut

ing horns. Roe bucks begin even earlier. The purpose of horn growth in winter, when the shortage of forage usually prevents the growth of body parts, is to have weapons in prime condition for spring or early summer in time for territorial contests. A pronghorn buck's horns might suffer damage during fighting while an occasional horn is torn free from the horn core.

However, to grow horns in winter requires that they are shed before winter. Pronghorns and roe bucks shed their head gear just before bucks join the large wintering herds of females, not very long after the rut in October. Peter Bromley proposed that shedding horns and diving into female herds increases security for bucks. The bucks, weakened by the rut and thus slower with less endurance in running than females, would become a predator's prime target. The bucks are not only recovering from exhaustion, but also from wounds. By looking like and mingling with females in large herds, the bucks blend into the herd and are no longer conspicuous to predators. Predators that are accustomed to the futility of chasing healthy females will not bother for long with a herd of females. When the black horns are shed, the horn cores look remarkably similar to ears. They are as long as the ears and covered with white hair except for the dark horn tip.

However, the male might assume the appearance of a female not only because of predators,

WHEN BUCKS BECOME territorial, they head for elevated positions to scan their huge territories for intruders. They locate places to see and to be seen.

but also to be accepted on equal terms within the female herd. That is, to become inconspicuous, the males must freely mingle with females. The females must not avoid males by giving them a big berth. Rather, the distance between females and hornless males must be equal on average. Only then does the male truly blend into the female herd. The bucks must be as unintimidating to females as possible, lest they are avoided or quickly left at the rear of the herd. We have here a case of female mimicry by males. This idea appears to apply not only to pronghorns, but to other ungulates as well. It is found in several species of deer, including mule deer, whitetails and caribou. Males shed their conspicuous antlers before becoming members of large female congregations. Caribou bulls even shed the conspicuous white neck manes. Similar to caribou, buffalo bulls shed much of their nuptial hair coat after the rut. Mule deer bucks go as far as to assume the crouched urination posture of the female.

Pronghorn bucks generally leave bachelor herds and establish territories in their third summer. They might occupy the

AFTER THE RUTTING SEASON, pronghorns congregate in large herds. The bucks, having shed their horn sheaths, resemble females and are integrated smoothly into this "selfish" herd. This is one of the most important security strategies in plains-dwelling ungulates — safety in packed numbers.

Establishing a territory is based on much bravado

territories of bucks that died, or create new territories by first establishing themselves between two territories. They strive to be geographically dominant wherever females prefer to feed.

Overt fighting in pronghorns is potentially very dangerous, as bucks wound and occasionally kill one another, and combat wounds are costly to heal. Consequently, natural selection favors a less costly means of one buck gaining the upper hand over another. Establishing a territory is thus based on much bravado, that is, conspicuous visual and vocal displays and copious marking of the land laid claim to. This is described well by David Kitchen's pioneering work on pronghorn behavior. As in other ruminants, pronghorn bucks show off to others frequently and at length. These antics are called dominance displays, and displaying bucks do get their way. A territorial

buck conspicuously occupies elevated points in the landscape, making himself conspicuous. Compared to bachelor bucks, his movements are crisp and expressive. He turns smartly and approaches incoming males from his vantage point. He stares at small bucks directly and might chase them off unceremoniously. Bucks chasing bucks may roar aggressively, and occasionally, bucks chasing does also roar. The territorial buck is more careful with big bucks than with yearlings. Rather than rush in, he will walk in and perform various displays.

BELOW, A BACHELOR HERD of bucks well before the rut and intensified animosity. During the rut, the black hairs on the subauricular gland might be flared and glistening with the gland's secretion, right. Bucks mark elevated objects such as the tops of bushes or dry twigs.

The territorial buck might vocalize when approaching other bucks. He has thus a territorial call. It begins with a snort, similar to an alarm snort. That, of course, attracts attention to him — as an alarm call must! This is quickly followed, however, by a series of short sounds of descending pitch and volume, which, to our ear, sound a little bit like wheezing laughter. When wheeze-calling, territorial bucks are excited, as indicated by the slight spread of the upper rump patch, which might also release scent from glands located there, and by an erection of the mane. This wheeze-call may also be uttered in courtship.

The territorial buck might not only wheeze call, but also grind his teeth and thrash shrubs vigorously with his horns. The other buck, par-

THIS RARE ALL-OUT CLASH between large males might eventually lead to injury and possibly death. In contrast to harmless sparring, these combatants, low over the ground to protect chest and belly, are straining maximally. Their horns allow locking, and thus wrestling and a test of strength. A third male rushes in to take advantage of the unprotected does.

Overt fighting is potentially very dangerous

O U S

ticularly if he is a territorial neighbor close to their mutual boundary, might respond in kind. The approach toward a potentially dangerous rival might be interrupted repeatedly by the territorial buck — and by his rival — by stopping and feeding. The territorial buck might swing broadside to large newcomers and erect the hair on the back of his neck and body, increasing his apparent size. He might walk, head low, parallel with a newcomer, as both assume this display. A very confident buck might also erect himself, then stand or walk stiffly and turn his head pointedly as if showing off the dark cheek patch below his ear, the location of his very smelly subauricular, or cheek, gland. Territorial bucks use this gland to mark tall vegetation within their territory. In

BUCKS IN RUT, below, might horn vegetation as done by so many horned and antlered animals. Right, territorial bucks signal possession of their territory by a ritual of scraping, urinating and defecating on one spot. Here, the buck is defecating, placing the fecal pellets between his hind hoofs.

enclosures, captive bucks might mark your finger with this gland if you stick it through the wire. Normally, a territorial buck picks a twig preferably at chest level, lowers his head, turns it till the secretion impregnated hair of the cheek gland touches the twig, and then rubs secretion on the twig with up and down motions. Gazelles have similar behaviors. However, they secrete marking fluids from the preorbital gland just ahead of the eye.

Territorial pronghorn bucks mark in many localities of their very large territory. These are quite variable in size, with the largest covering over a square mile and the smallest covering about 50 acres. The average territory is between 120 and 160 acres.

Territorial pronghorn bucks also mark in another fashion, which is astoundingly similar to that of Asian and African gazelles and dwarf antelopes. The buck stops, sniffs and paws the ground alternately with his front hoofs. Then he steps over the pawed spots, stretches his hind legs to the back and urinates. As soon as he has finished urinating, he steps forward with his hind legs, deeply arches his back and defecates on the same spot. Like marking with the cheek gland, this type of marking is spread over the territory and might be renewed periodically. Large males might urinate and defecate over the spot where a subordinate urinated and defecated.

Less-than-confident bucks express their mood only too clearly. They may look directly at an approaching territorial buck without replying to his dominance displays. A confident buck pinches in his tail, depresses the hairs on his rump patch and neck, raises the hair about the median gland on his back, folds his ears back, looks past his rival and walks slowly and stiffly. A loser, on the other hand, erects his tail, his neck mane, the upper third of his rump patch, raises his head, puts his ears up into a neutral position and walks quickly without stiffness. Most 3-year-old bucks are territorial or serious contenders, while yearlings and 2-year-olds are found in bachelor groups. However, bachelor or not, they do try to breed females. Among themselves, sparring and mounting by one small bachelor buck to another is not uncommon. Sparring, however, occurs also among does. Does usually are equipped with small horns and use them to threaten or butt away other does from favored feeding or bedding sites.

Territoriality is but one manner in which males advertise their superiority and attract females. The attraction for females of a fine, confident buck lies not only in superior genes, as one too readily might assume, but rather in a more mundane benefit: Dominant bucks keep bachelors away which, by courting frequently, would harass females and impose increase maintenance costs. Maintenance costs are deducted from the

A TERRITORIAL BUCK vocalizing during courtship. This wheeze call is a very loud sign of a confident male.

reproductive account and thus the biological success of the females. To maximize her reproductive fitness, it behooves the female to find good forage sites where she can feed, rest and raise her young with as little disruption by sex-driven males as possible. That location is the territory of a large, dominant male.

There are other manners for males to declare their superiority and attract females. The main alternative is for males to form dominance hierarchies. In this system, males decorate themselves with costly luxury organs such as large horns or antlers, as well as elaborate hair coats like those found in caribou or bison. The development of luxury organs speaks of the male's general health, his ability to find superior food, and the chances he takes with predators. Luxury organs reflect surplus energy above maintenance that a male accumulates. Clearly, the healthier a male, the lower his costs of fighting parasites, diseases or injuries, and the more resources for fancy horns and hair coats. Also, good food in very secure localities has normally been removed by females, because they value security above good food. That means some of the best food is found where predators are more likely to be successful. Consequently, to grow superior luxury organs, a male has to take more chances with predators by seeking out superior feeding sites that are not very secure. The advantage of territoriality to a plains dweller adapted to speed is that it need not compete with

luxury organs. Highly functional horns for fighting need not be big. Nor does the territorial buck need to fatten as do males with a hierarchical mating system because his site of good food and breeding are the same. Roaming hierarchical males, however, must ensure a secure supply of energy, or fat, no matter where breeding activity erupts. Territoriality, over all, appears to be less costly in energy and nutrients than male breeding hierarchies because there is no costly race for bigger luxury organs, larger fat deposits or larger bodies. Territoriality is better suited to species-rich mature ecosystems, male hierarchies to

immature, early, disturbed ecosystems or wherever competition for high-quality forage resources is modest. North America, having lost its species-rich, diverse Ice Age fauna, currently has a surfeit of species with male breeding hierarchies. Today, it is a species-poor, immature fauna made up of a few North American survivors and new Siberian (Beringian) immigrants.

Bucks persuade females to stay on their territories in several ways. One trick is to have females give birth on the territory. That should ensure not only the female's loyalty to

AFTER A BRIEF COURTSHIP, the estrous female invites the territorial buck to copulate. She stands, raises her tail and moves ahead of him.

the birth area in her first year of birth, which makes her available as a mate during the subsequent mating season, but very likely ensures her loyalty to the territory in subsequent years as well. That's the best explanation why bucks herd females toward their territory before fawning — four to five months before the mating season — a discovery made through the careful quantitative work of David W. Kitchen.

Otherwise, the buck holds females by the territo-

A doe attempting to leave will find her way blocked

ry's quality as a feeding site, by minimizing harassment from bachelor bucks, and by actively constraining the females' movements. That's herding. A doe attempting to leave will find her way blocked by the threatening territorial buck, blocking her way broadside with his body, his head lowered almost to the ground. Most maneuvering by the buck is done at a walk as he keeps himself strategically positioned between the females and the nearest border of his territory. However, females may be persistent in trying to leave the area. The territorial buck may then herd much more forcefully, chasing the females back to the interior of the territory. Such runs may be long, taking the form of long loops. A buck intercepting and aggressively herding does may utter the same roar as a buck chasing a defeated rival. Herding is overtly aggressive and dangerous as the buck might attempt to gore females that he intercepts. Herding by bucks might also include dominance displays such as thrashing vegetation, urination-defecation and marking with the cheek gland. In theory, that ought to be attractive to the females as it characterizes territoriality and dominance, which from the female's perspective should be attractive attributes. Females that persist in escaping do so eventually. The buck focuses on one departing female at a time and tries to round her up. In the meantime, the others keep moving off. The herd sometimes splits into several groups that might move off in different directions.

Bucks must not only herd females, but also persuade them to stay. This requires courtship. The courting buck approaching does from a distance might utter a high pitch whine, which soon descends in pitch and terminates in a series of deep guttural sounds. The buck's head is held high, the hair over the median gland is erect, as is the mane on his neck, and he advances with short prancing steps. As he closes in on the doe, he starts moving his head laterally back and forth, usually four or five times, sometimes less, sometimes more. While head waving, he audibly flicks his tongue in and out and loudly smacks his lips. These sounds are similar to the exaggerated sounds of a suckling fawn. Apparently, the courting pronghorn buck uses baby mimicry in courting, parasitizing the female's maternal emotions, holding her back, which in principle is also done by other courting ruminants. He might also display his cheek patch from an erected head. In short, when courting, the territorial buck uses quite different signals toward the female than when herding. There is considerable variation in courtship approaches and the performance of various signals. Courtship may also be disrupted when another buck moves in, and the territorial buck moves off to evict the rival.

In response to courtship, females might duck down deeply and urinate, and the buck might then test the urine with a lip curl. In this behavior, the buck takes some urine into his mouth,

HAREM HERDING BUCKS chase back and posture to females trying to leave the territory. The buck not only postures visibly, but also projects his territorial scent via a widely flared subauricular gland, bottom photo.

Bucks must persuade females to stay, which requires courtship

curls back the upper lip and exposes a small orifice and channel in his upper palate, leading to the Jacobson's or vomero-nasal organ. We suspect that the sensory ciliated epithelium within this small sensory pouch signals the female's sexual receptivity to some hormone or breakdown product in the urine. While the buck is lip-curling, the doe may move away. After lip-curling, the buck might urinate and defecate over the urine spot left by the female. Unreceptive does avoid the buck. They move off in a slight crouch, head lowered, occasionally shaking their head. They also place obstacles between themselves and the buck.

Females in heat do not avoid the buck, but look at him and might spread their hind legs and raise the tail. The buck displays the cheek patch and moves with exaggerated short steps. The doe becomes so bold as to sniff the buck's cheek patch. She remains standing with her tail raised while the buck touches her with his muzzle on the croup, and then with his chest on her haunches. He may then slide up on her and walk on the hind legs in contact with the doe. After a few pelvic movements, the buck suddenly dips his head toward the female, then uncoils, throwing his head high while bounding upward with his haunches as copulation is achieved. The buck's hind legs leave the ground completely. Thereafter, the doe leaves the buck, losing inter-

EVEN WHEN UNDISTURBED, the guarding buck is ever alert and vigilant. He can grow impatient and attempt to mount the resting doe.

est almost at once. Repeat copulations aren't normally observed.

During the period of receptivity, territorial bucks may vanish while bachelors invade the apparently abandoned territory and chase females. Closer research revealed that territorial males are in hiding with a receptive female. After the female is bred, the territorial buck fetches another into hiding — leaving bachelor bucks to chase nonreceptive females. The point of defending a large territory is apparently to prevent other males from knowing the secret hide-aways where the courting couple retire. Only the largest territorial males will succeed in denying all access to rivals. They, in turn, might move onto a lesser buck's territory, defeat him, but leave him in possession of the territory, which the victor, of course, scouts out. Thus, the territory is linked to a system of dominance hierarchies that parallels the territorial system and permits the most dominant buck's breeding privileges on a rival's territory. That appears to be a unique feature of pronghorn society.

Pronghorns are pliable in their biology, changing as circumstances warrant. Yes, pronghorn bucks are territorial, but not all. On dry ranges, where concentrated feeding sites are few, pronghorn bucks abandon territorial behavior and defend females as they come into heat. The breeding system is now hierarchical. Pronghorns are not rigid about such matters, territories are dandy, but one can also do without and still breed.

CHAPTER 5

THE PRAIRIE'S CHANGING LANDSCAPE

Today's prairie is not the environment of the pronghorn's past, but an artifact of early and current human activities. What is today prairie was then a rich mosaic of meadows, shrubs and tree groves.

What is today

I remember how excited Peter Bromley was when he saw how well pronghorn biology fit prairie ecology. Because of what pronghorns can do, they could deal with the severe droughts that haunted the prairie periodically, the huge wild fires that so frequently swept the grasslands in the none-too-distant past, the sudden snowfalls that mired wildlife and livestock alike in the severest of winters, and the terrible blizzards that scoured the plains mercilessly during Arctic cold snaps. Bromley's doctoral dissertation put the pieces of the puzzle together. However, good scientist that he was, he also saw that matters did not always fit as neatly as they ought to. Indeed, it could not, for today's prairie is not the environment of the pronghorn's past, but an artifact of early and current human activities in North American. However, previously, nobody had come to that insight, and we regarded the prairie as an environment little changed, in principle, from the distant past. When herds of

MOSAIC
prairie was then a rich mosaic
of meadows, shrubs and tree groves

For about 200 in North

THE BUFFALO WAS BIG BROTHER to the pronghorn, right. Both nearly vanished for good, and both have returned through dedicated conservation efforts. Above, a buck, rump patch flared, eye cocked to rear, runs to catch up with a larger buck.

horses, camels and elephants still roamed North America, what is today prairie was then a rich mosaic of meadows, shrubs and tree groves. The fact that the pronghorn can handle today's bleak prairie speaks to the adaptability of this smart, little creature.

When the pronghorn was first discovered in the Western world early in the 19th century, when its numbers were so large they might have exceeded those of the buffalo, pronghorn herds were seen not only among herds of bison and groups of light-colored gray wolves, but also among big herds of mustangs. The mustang congregations were, clearly, not "natural," as horses re-entered North America with Columbus. However, the big herds of bison were not entirely natural, either. For about 200 years, nature in North America had truly run wild. In the century after 1492 A.D., massive mortality befell North American Indians. European diseases and genocide swiftly decimated native tribes and lifted the heavy hand of the red man off the continent's landscape and wildlife. The sheer abundance of wildlife and the well-documented spread of bison and elk between about 1600 to 1800 A.D., was caused by the scarcity of humans, who had

previously cropped wildlife closely on the continent for nearly 10,000 years.

Since their entry into North America about 12,000 years ago, American Indians had no trivial impact on North America's ecology. The destruction of North America's native megafauna by human hand 7,000 to 12,000 years ago profoundly altered the landscape. Gone were the huge elephants, mastodons and ground sloths that kept tree growth trimmed and dispersed. Gone were the giant peccaries that plowed the ground. Gone were the myriad species of horses that clipped the grasses and sedges close to the ground, preparing the plant communities for exploitation by smaller-bodied species. In their place stepped huge, destructive wildfires. These fires haunted early settlers of the prairies, and they haunt forests to this day.

When the tree-and-grass-removing megafauna was in place, wildfires were few and small. When the megafauna was removed, fuel accumulated and trees grew virtually unchecked, and wildfires could burn hot and long over wide areas. It might well have been the huge wildfires and the severe ecological changes they imposed that removed so many native species from North America. It might also be that humans coming early to this continent set much of it ablaze — deliberately. Hot fires would have stripped woody vegetation from the land, dried out soils and impoverished them of nutrients, removing biodiversity as well as habitat diversity. Thus, long before the Europeans came, ancient man in

120 | ANTELOPE COUNTRY

NATURE

years, nature
America had truly run wild

North America had inadvertently ensured that a big ecological artifact hit the landscape year in year out: huge wildfires in grassland and forests.

I suspect this is what changed North American plant associations profoundly during our current interglacial period. It suggests that our landscape is vegetated atypically even for an interglacial period. We expect the landscape to be vegetated differently during glacial and interglacial periods. Whether differences exist during Ice Age and historic times is a subject of scientific debate. Even though parties to the debate might not agree on much, they do agree that plant communities on this continent are now vastly different.

Native people learned to use fires to alter the landscape to their advantage long before the days of Columbus. In regions with good soils and climate, they also developed sophisticated agriculture and great civilizations. In ecologically poorer regions, hunter-gatherers barely eked out an existence as evidenced by their

archaeological remains and the small size and asymmetry of their skeletons. The big game they brought in revealed that large beasts like elk, bison and moose were quite uncommon. The depletion of these large species was likely a consequence of the great hunger that characterized much of North America in pre-Columbian times. Hunter-gatherers routinely crushed deer jaw and other bones to boil out the last drop of fat. Today, elders recall that such practices were done only when food was extremely scarce. Pre-Colombian North America was not a wilderness paradise. It was such a place for a mere two centuries between the lifting of the red man's hand and the imposition of the even heavier white man's hand. Wilderness is a post-Columbian artifact of European colonization.

The effects of these processes on the prairie were profound, even where the prairie was not plowed under. Where it was plowed under, droughts destroyed the exposed soils, generating "black blizzards" when the hot winds blew. Previously, with a fire-conditioned grass and herb sward in place, droughts were probably much more bearable. The terrible effect of blizzards might, in part, be a consequence of the lack of obstruction, hence the wind's ability to saturate the first 10 feet above the ground with high-speed ice crystals and flying dirt. And, the lack of obstructing vegetation is historically a function of prairie fires. Big, hot fires remove all tree and shrub growth and burn the soil's upper layers — ideal conditions for grasses.

The Ice Age megafauna might have crunched and toppled trees, but by limiting wildfires, they also ensured a wider distribution of trees and shrubs. They also recycled much of the woody biomass into fertile dung, which they transported and deposited away from feeding areas. In this process, they redistributed nutrients. Huge herbivores were also redistributors of seeds ensuring affected plants were widely distributed. All that would have made for a much more savannah-like landscape on what was classic prairie. Plant fossil data support the notion of widespread, moist savannah during the late glacial period. Moreover, the large herbivores' trails, hoofprints, dung heaps and pawed-up resting pits generated a micro-ecology that must have teemed with insects, small birds and mammals. At least that is what is

THIS BUCK EXHIBITS an excellent illustration of worn winter hair about to be shed. Note also the thickened horn bases, swollen with blood, at the end of the horn growth.

suggested by the large number of small- and medium-sized hawks and falcon species that went extinct along with the megafauna. Such a high diversity of raptors and condors, each probably quite specialized ecologically, can only exist where there is a rich and diverse prey base. The megaherbivores thus had a long ecological coattail that vanished with their demise beginning about 11,500 years ago.

We know little about pronghorns before the beginning of the 19th century, although they dazzled early travelers with their speed, beauty and numbers. Archaeological sites disclose few pronghorns. They are outnumbered by deer and mountain sheep. However, that does not mean pronghorn were scarce, but only that they were hard to hunt and not much of a prize after the hunt. Pronghorns are lean, and native hunters craved fat. Without fat or adequate carbohydrates from plant sources, lean meat is not much good as food. Deer and sheep are much fatter than pronghorns. The abundant remains of fish, reptiles and small mammals in archaeological remains — in contrast to the scarcity of large-bodied animals like elk, bison and moose — indicate a general scarcity of these seasonally fat mammals. Thus archaeology does not inform us much about pronghorns.

Scholars of past native cultures noted that pronghorn were not a common food item. They were taken occasionally, but hunting pronghorns in earlier days was difficult. Bison, clearly, were a much more rewarding game to hunt. Still, there are indications that skilled native bowmen took pronghorns at watering holes. Others, in a tribal effort, built low-fenced corrals and maneuvered pronghorns into them where the animals were clubbed to death. Only low fences were required because pronghorns, for all their ability to leap horizontally over great chasms, do not usually jump over even low vertical obstacles. Pronghorns can jump up, but usually don't. That's their Achilles' heel.

Although large-scale prairie fires, severe droughts and possibly severe blizzards are in part artifacts of human making, and thus not natural, the high reproductive rate of pronghorns and their propensity to cover long distances quickly probably enhanced survival and allowed pronghorns rapid recovery from severe mortalities. However, these attributes were probably evolved in response to the severe predation pronghorns experienced dur-

ing the Pleistocene. Yet pronghorns will drift before major winter storms, and some bands do escape the worst snowfalls. The propensity to roam is characteristic of cursorial plains-dwellers. The hapless response of pronghorns to deep, loose snow indicates the species evolved where such calamities were rare. This is supported by the paleontological record that suggests a warmth-loving fauna south of the big ice sheaths during continental glaciations.

What little evidence there is of Ice Age prong-horns is of large-bodied individuals. That suggests pronghorn experienced moist, long-lasting, fertile conditions during summer. Pronghorns on the northern rim of their geographic distribution — in Montana or the Canadian prairies — grow to a similar size as did their Ice Age ancestors, indicating good conditions for pregnant and lactating females. However, the frequent decimation of Northern pronghorns by severe winters indicates they reached their limits to cope with winter. They have thus a heaven and hell routine: heaven in summer and hell in winter.

Severe droughts can devastate pronghorns. Populations are not only affected by severe mortality, but survivors do not reproduce well after severe droughts. Such are initiated by severe, desiccating winds that blow with little respite. The soil and vegetation dries, and both might drift across the land in dense black clouds. Grit covers everything. Every drought this century saw pronghorn numbers plummet. Water in fair abundance is thus essential for good pronghorn populations. Not surprisingly, the rich flush of grasses and forbs that follows

RIGHT, AN ALERT DOE after giving birth. Below, winter kill. Great cold, the energy drain of deep snow, food buried and hard to reach, snow crusts that wound legs and the vigilance of hungry predators all take their toll.

the snow melt in Northern prairies leads to the highest rates of reproduction and body growth among pronghorns — except for some small populations in their southern distribution of Texas, Arizona and New Mexico. These herds live along permanent water courses and enjoy the diversity of native plant phenology generated by deeply incised river breaks and grasslands that fan out beyond the breaks.

Deep snow and cold are death to pronghorns. Their fat reserves are low at the best of times, and they need access to nutritious forbs. Deep snow forces pronghorns to work hard by digging for food below the snow, and it hinders speedy flight. Once pronghorns are weakened by malnutrition, their speed and endurance diminishes. Coyotes — particularly pack-hunting coyotes — might become quite successful catching adult pronghorns. In deep snow, pronghorns also fall victim to modern transportation methods. They might crowd onto cleared railway lines and be killed by the dozen by trains. Along some highways, cleared shoulders expose grasses and forbs that attract pronghorns. Here they can fall victims to motor vehicles. In deep-snow winters, pronghorns might move into the fringes of human settlements where they become quite tame, but also fall victim to traffic and domestic dogs.

hell in winter

COYO

Coyotes may become quite successful

catching adul

TES
pronghorn

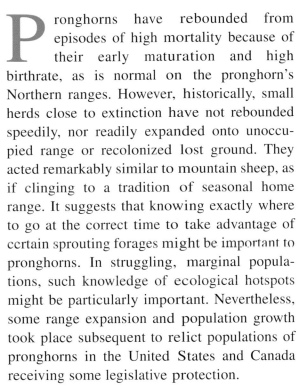

P ronghorns have rebounded from
episodes of high mortality because of
their early maturation and high
birthrate, as is normal on the pronghorn's
Northern ranges. However, historically, small
herds close to extinction have not rebounded
speedily, nor readily expanded onto unoccu-
pied range or recolonized lost ground. They
acted remarkably similar to mountain sheep, as
if clinging to a tradition of seasonal home
range. It suggests that knowing exactly where
to go at the correct time to take advantage of
certain sprouting forages might be important to
pronghorns. In struggling, marginal populations, such knowledge of ecological hotspots
might be particularly important. Nevertheless,
some range expansion and population growth
took place subsequent to relict populations of
pronghorns in the United States and Canada
receiving some legislative protection.

Pronghorns fare well under today's conditions, as indicated by their general abundance.
Thus, their adaptations fit — by and large.
However, that's an accident, just as it is an
accident that elk are quite well adapted to
North America. The elk is, after all, a rather
recent immigrant to North America. It is doing
well here because of absence of food competition from other co-adapted deer.

In Asia, modern elk of the same type as our
wapiti, are narrowly confined to aspen forests
and alpine and subalpine grasslands. They do
not enjoy the ubiquitous distribution that elk

THE COYOTE, UNLIKE the gray wolf, is also an old
American, and a predator with a long experience
hunting pronghorns. When coyotes hunt in packs,
they become very efficient at killing prey. Where
single coyotes fail, the group succeeds.

enjoy in North America in prairies, foothills,
Eastern deciduous and Pacific rain forest, and
even on sage brush flats. In Siberia, although
advanced elk are confined to the highlands,
different subspecies of red deer and elk exploit
the valley bottoms.

Elk entered North America into an ecological
vacuum left by the destruction of its megafauna.
Pronghorns also benefited from this ecological
vacuum and became abundant. That is, pronghorns are not common in the fossil record during
the ice ages, but become abundant subsequent to
megafaunal extinction. The same can be said of
deer and peccaries, and is probably true of black
bears, coyotes and mountain lions as well. After
the giant peccaries vanished, today's small, primitive peccary expanded its range northward into
what today is the United States. It is as if the old,
diverse native fauna of North America kept a lid
on the abundance of deer, coyotes, pronghorns,
black bears, and peccaries. Once the lid of competition and severe predation came off, these species
prospered, as did newly arrived species coming
from Siberia — elk, bison, grizzly bear, gray wolf
and man. And that is why an ecological study of
pronghorns tells us only a fraction of what there is
to know about pronghorns. One has to dig into history. After all, pronghorns are history!

CHAPTER 6

BORN TO RUN: A FAWN'S LIFE

In spring, the prairies welcome new life.

But those same prairies also contain

death traps for newborn pronghorn.

A fawn's very survival depends on not

being seen, heard or smelled.

They are born to run fast, see far

and — as young — to hide.

A baby pronghorn's liquid eyes and baby face are beguiling in their sheer innocent childishness, and yet each pronghorn's life begins with murder, with fratricide to be precise. It is a remarkable story, which was deciphered by Professor Bart O'Gara of the Cooperative Wildlife Research Unit of the University of Montana. Several researchers were on the trail, heading the same direction, but it was Professor O'Gara who finally made sense of it all.

Pronghorn females normally give birth to twins. During pregnancy, each of the kids occupies one of her two uterine horns. However, early in gestation there are more embryos floating free in the lumen. There might be half a dozen or more. Female pronghorns super-ovulate at breeding. That is, their ovaries release a burst of mature eggs for fertilization by the buck's sperms. The zygotes forming from egg and sperm soon attach to the lining of the uterine walls, each to begin the life of a pronghorn.

In the words of O'Gara: "Egg and sperm soon reach the uterus as tiny, football-shaped blastocysts. They rapidly elongate into thread-like tubes about 5 inches (13 cm) long and the diameter of a 6-pound-test (2.7 kg) monofilament fishing line. The tube walls, which will become the fetal membranes, are only one cell thick, and the embryo-to-be is a tiny ball of cells on one wall. The Y-shaped uterus is still active from hormones related to ovulation, and the thread-stage blastocysts are kneaded together, often tangling.

One-fourth to one-third generally perish. Next, tubal walls thicken and grow villi that implant into the uterine lining. In each uterine horn, one will reach a better blood supply with its villi than do its siblings."

And that's when the fight for space begins between surviving embryos. Although many might be initially implanted, only two will survive, and the others will perish. The survivors help the perishing along. They grow projections from their fetal membranes, which pierce or dis-

place the bodies and membranes of the competing embryos. The tip of each projection dissolves the strange embryo. The survivors thus kill off brothers and sisters within the uterus. There is room for only two, and two kids are normally born.

Birth and early life are terribly dangerous periods in the pronghorn's life. To start with, females in the last weeks of pregnancy are not expected to be as fleet of foot as

A BABY PRONGHORN. Look at its large, black eyes that promise to one day see far into the prairie and protect self and herd. Note its uniform color, resembling that of earth, rock, dead wood or cow chips. A big adventure lies ahead.

barren does. Pronghorn kids are large, and there are two inside the female! They are a burden, and although this has not been investigated, where it has been observed — such as with axis deer, a beautiful spotted deer native to India, that were preyed on by swift, pack-hunting red dogs —

**ABOVE, A PREGNANT PRONGHORN doe bloated
with young. Birth is timed to coincide with the
growth of nutritious forage. Right, a pronghorn doe
with prolapsed uterus, a rare, fatal event.**

heavily gravid does were more likely to be run
down and caught than other does. The big eyes of
the pronghorn females might come in handy to
spot predators a long way off, thus allowing them
to take evasive action early.

During the birth process and shortly thereafter,
females are totally vulnerable to predators.
Consequently, it is sensible that they isolate
themselves to minimize attention and to find a
concealed locality that is not normally visited by
predators. Females that frequented wide open
flats might move to rocky ridges before giving
birth. In today's national parks, such secure spots
might be close to bustling tourist activity,
because coyotes, wolves and mountain lions normally avoid human's. As indicated earlier, pronghorns are brainy!

Away from tourists, gravid pronghorn females
tend to choose hollows in elevated locations, just
as bucks do when harassed in hunting season.
Here pronghorns are difficult to find — unless one
is clued in. Such localities are normally off the
beaten paths. They are relatively safe, because
predators are not likely to look where they previously found no prey. An odd birth site for pronghorns are river islands. Southern pronghorns living in dry conditions were observed moving to
green spots before fawning. Clearly, good feed
close to where fawns are born is very important.

Shortly before birth, when the first contrac-
tions set in, one might still be able to see the
fawns kicking inside the female. Her belly-line
changes in anticipation of birth. The female
might be agitated and aggressive toward others.
Even after the amniotic fluid has emerged, a disturbed female might still withdraw the bladder
and run off to give birth elsewhere. The time of
high or total vulnerability — from the first con-
tractions until the female departs with her two
newborns — lasts about six hours.

As the fawns are born, the doe does her part to
ensure a rapid onset of their vital abilities. First
she removes and consumes the birth membranes
from each fawn, and then licks the birth fluid
from their pelts. In essence, she quickly removes
all visual and olfactory evidence of the births.
Birds of prey might spot the expelled placenta
and, in descending to scavenge it, might attract
attention to the birth site. Terrestrial predators
might smell the birth fluids and home in on the
birth site. Removing placenta and birth fluid thus
protects the fawns. Drying their wavy hair coat
also ensures the hair begins to insulate the fawns.
This is a necessity because fawns are born early
in the year when cold weather is frequent.

Pronghorn kids must be large enough and insu-
lated enough to avoid rapid cooling of their bodies. However, during cold, wet weather, this
might not be achieved. Snowstorms at birthing
times might kill a lot of pronghorn fawns.
Sometimes such weather all but eliminates a
fawn crop. The fawns die of hypothermia, an

process, and shortly thereafter, females are totally vulnerable

The fawns survival depends
on not being seen, heard

acute danger for all small-bodied Northern ruminants. Such unlucky fawns might be found later virtually mummified. Fawns in captivity became ill in cold weather.

The female also massages and stimulates by vigorously licking the fawn's anal and urinary orifices. This is vital for the normal voiding by the fawns. In captive fawns, this procedure needs to be imitated by whomever cares for the fawns to ensure normal defecation and urination. Under natural conditions, the mother's licking stimulates voiding. The female then quickly ingests and licks what the fawn voided. This is another procedure in the perpetual effort to minimize clues about the fawns' whereabouts. The fawns'

MATURE GOLDEN EAGLES are capable predators of pronghorns. They will not only overpower fawns, but on occasion kill adults by striking panic-stricken pronghorns and riding them to death. Below, the ducking fawn resembles a shapeless mass.

very lives thus depend on their cleanliness. In their first week of life, fawns apparently produce little scent of their own. Most coyotes move downwind past bedded fawns without detecting them, but there is enough scent that, occasionally, one does detect a fawn — and so might domestic dogs with good noses. Nevertheless, there is a protective function in scent reduction and it is found in other ruminants that have newborns that hide. The fawns' survival depends on not being seen, heard or smelled.

Shortly after birth, the fawns are still quite clumsy on their legs. As yet, their security does not depend on dashing off at high speed. That is still to come. A fawn's security now depends on a sophisticated way to hide, which was discovered by Peter Bromley. Close, detailed observation and an open mind paid off. He noted, as have many others, that fawns move off on their own after birth. The mother follows, but does not encourage or discourage her twins in any way. Each fawn — on its own and guided by instinct — searches for an appropriate place to lie down. The fawns know exactly what to do, and that knowledge comes as part of their hereditary endowment. Such vital functions as correctly hiding right after birth cannot be left to some chancy learning process, but must be available at once. Therefore,

IVAL

or smelled

The fawns

how to hide must come as inborn knowledge at birth. Let's watch and see what a newborn pronghorn does.

Standing close to its mother, the newborn is quite conspicuous, at least to human eyes. First one twin, and then the other, moves off head held low to the ground, looking about as if searching for the right spot. There might be short, lush green grass at the birth site. Here the fawns move about as if dissatisfied with the surroundings. Suddenly, one fawn has vanished from view, and then — equally quick and surprising — so does the other. The cover of short green grass cannot have swallowed them. Where are they?

It takes a keen eye well-schooled in detecting detail to see through it all. Yes, observation takes practice and training. We now detect one of the fawns. As expected, the little fellow is down, head to the ground and curled up. However, there is more to it: The fawn has placed its body partly over a dry batch of buffalo dung. With its gray coat, the fawn fits perfectly with the dried splatter of dung. Its body contours are broken up and fused with the dung's contours. Visually, the fawn is part of the dung heap. However, because buffalo dung heaps and the dung heaps of other ungulates are common where pronghorns are found, but fawns are rare, it would take a prodigious effort for carnivores to inspect every dung heap in hope of finding a newborn.

DAY-OLD FAWNS are a little clumsy on their legs, but they try to exercise by running. What else is more important to a pronghorn?

are still quite clumsy on their legs

CLUMSY

Standing close to its mother, is quite

the newborn
conspicuous, at least to human eyes.

But where is fawn No. 2? No, he is not part of a buffalo chip, at least not of any buffalo chip in sight. Yet he, too, was in the open just before disappearing. But watch, there is a little patch of gravelly rock protruding from the green sward. Is the rock patch not a little larger than it was a moment ago? Indeed, there is the second fawn. Its body outlines are broken by the gravel patch. The fawn blends in to become part of the rock. Both fawns are not obstructed by any cover, and thus in full view — especially from above. Golden eagles will sail by high above, screening each square inch of prairie for prey. Fawns are eagle food, as we know only too well from direct observation. Yet it is likely that the great eagle will sail by without deciphering the outlines of a few buffalo chips and rock patches as squatting pronghorn fawns.

In earlier epochs there were far more large birds of prey in North American skies. A fawn's innate search for something to lie against that breaks its outline from above might have evolved because of the great number of large predatory bird species pronghorns had to deal with. In their Ice Age past, there were keen-eyed golden eagles, bald eagles and ravens, as well as many now-extinct condors, eagles and giant hawks. They were the greatest threat by day. At night, the terrestrial carnivores took over. However, a scentless, motionless baby pronghorn hunkered against a big pile of smelly mammoth dung probably had a

IN THEIR FIRST three days of life, fawns bond with their mothers. They develop so quickly that they are soon next to impossible to catch by hand.

good chance of escaping detection. And with the many species of large herbivores on North America's savannahs and plains, there must have been a lot of dung piles by horses, bison, camels and other beasts. Today, pronghorn fawns also might choose to hunker down beside a sage brush or beside some grass or tall herbs. That might, however, be today's response — choosing the second best — in the absence of diverse dung heaps.

Hiding is a very successful survival strategy that has independently evolved by many antelope and deer. In every case studied so far, it is the fawn that seeks a place to hide, unassisted by the mother. Loud sounds, but especially a commotion staged by mothers, cause fawns to drop motionless to the ground. Pronghorn females run at potential enemies. Small predators, up to the size of coyotes, are attacked by the female with spirit and vigor. Large predators, humans included, are treated to distraction displays in which the female — not unlike some nesting birds — feigns injury, evoking a follow response by the predator, luring it ever farther from her fawns. The fawns' high-pitched bleats might attract does, but also bucks from a quarter mile away or more. Newborn fawns handled by humans were not deserted by the female.

In their first few days of life outside the uterus, fawns learn to identify their mother. Newborns will stumble after a man, but not fawns several days old. In fact, 3-day-old fawns are already hard to catch by hand and impossible by the fourth day. The females

leave the general vicinity where their fawns are hidden, but keep in visual contact and are ever ready to return and avert danger. With hiders, the suckling periods are long and well-spaced initially (30 to 90 seconds), but become short and frequent when the fawns follow their dam (5 to 15 per day). Thus, does moving with fawns produce little milk at any one time. Each female suckles only her young and punishes strange fawns that try. Fawns grow rapidly on the female's very rich milk. To grow to surviv-

able size is the goal. If all goes well, fawns on a good range will almost match their mother in size when winter arrives. Experience with captive pronghorns has shown that milk from domestic cows is far too diluted for pronghorn fawns. Lactation lasts three to 3½ months. The fawns nibble plants by 7 days old and feed more or less regularly by 3 weeks old. They are weaned at summer's end, just before the rut.

Fawns join the female at 6 days old when their ability to run fast and smooth has matured. Soon they are little speed demons that might race ahead of their sprinting mothers. They will still drop from sight during flight and squat motionless on the ground till danger is past and their mother comes to pick them up. They shed their juvenile coat at 7 to 10 days old when their rump patch turns white. They flash this rump patch when escaping at a dead run, but then drop from sight, a trick they retain for the first month of life. A fawn's rump patch is very accentuated. As fawns become competent followers, the females might switch feeding grounds and leave the general birth area.

Fawns love to play! And that is very important for the proper growth of bones, muscles, sinews and nerves, and it creates a competent, confident pronghorn. Consequently, play is common from the first week after birth till about 6 months old when winter sets in. Pronghorn fawns readily race into rock outcroppings where they bounce about sure-footedly. They might also push each other off rocks. When hard-pressed as adults, pronghorns might seek security in elevation and cliffs. Fawns like to join others and form gangs during play.

Security strategies and tactics appear to be a matter of hard, unbending inheritance, which we discovered in experimental hybrid studies with deer. I suspect its no different with pronghorns.

TWINS, WHICH ARE NORMAL for pronghorns, stay and rest together. Ever alert, they can jump up and dash off in a split second.

CHAPTER 7

RETURN OF THE PRONGHORN

The demise of the pronghorn was rapid.
And today, although some ranchers cuss
the pronghorn, few realize how much
efffort, good will and money went into
returning it from the edge of extinction.

The pronghorn was little brother to the buffalo, and little brother almost shared the fate of his big brother. However, while efforts to restore pronghorns were not as dramatic or as publicized as those to restore bison, they were ultimately more successful. The problem with bison conservation is that it got stuck halfway and only occasionally went to completion. That is, in most localities, bison are kept behind fences, and that's not good enough. In few places do bison face predation by wolves and bears, which is essential to keep the bison's evolved antipredator adaptations in fighting trim. In evolution, it's use it or loose it. Consequently,

to adequately maintain a species for posterity, it needs to be exposed to native plants, climates and predators. On this point, as far as pronghorns go, there is little to complain about. Pronghorns are well-exposed to bobcats, coyotes, wolves and cougars, as well as to a full range of modern hazards. Gray wolves of the prairie no longer hunt pronghorns except where reintroduced in Yellowstone National Park, but it is questionable if they ever did so effectively in the past. Gray wolves are Siberian "snow dogs" with oversized soft paws, which are recent immigrants to North America. They are known for endurance, not speed. One might also question if their big, soft

INDANCE
once-endangered species
restored to abundance by human hand

PROSPECTS FOR PRONGHORNS were once dark indeed, but diligent conservation efforts paid off.

paws are good tools for hard, cacti-studded prairie surfaces. Pronghorns are doing well, but only because we, through clever and good management, got them back to reasonable abundance and distribution. Pronghorns today are a once-endangered species restored to abundance by human hand.

It was not an easy task.

The demise of little brother was rapid. In the 1830s, paddle-wheelers on major rivers contributed to the pronghorn's decline. In the 1860s, it was railway lines and the rapid development of

firearms. And then, an unbridled faith in the dollar and utter freedom to plunder the continent's wealth coupled with a military policy to deprive native people of wildlife by forcing them onto reservations. The West opened up for settlement, and big markets in the large cities devoured wildlife — songbirds included. All of these factors collectively helped exterminate North America's wildlife, and were virtually successful by the turn of the century. Judge Caton notes in the 1870s that pronghorns were extraordinarily common in California only 25 years before, but were exterminated by the time he wrote. In the central Great Plains, they hung on longer. As bison declined, so other big-game species were turned on. In winter, frozen pronghorn carcasses were stacked like cordwood along railway lines to be shipped east to urban centers. Although bison fell victim to a well-executed policy to deny plains tribes their bases of operation against the Army and settlers, the pronghorn was a mere "by-catch" of this campaign. As Teddy Roosevelt related, big-game species disappeared sequentially from the plains, depending on how easily they could be procured and how rewarding it was to kill them. It appears that, in 1867, after Army commanders decided on this covert campaign against wildlife, it took about two decades to bring silence to the prairie. Bleached bones of bison lay scattered over the land as mute testimony of their former abundance, until even the bones were sold, gathered and hauled away by the boxcar to be used to refine sugar.

To maintain a
to be exposed

A BUCK KILLED IN ACTION. Birds, magpies in this case, are often the first to spot and profit from a fresh carcass. These birds have pecked out the eye and removed the highly nutritious fat pad deep in the eye socket. Right, the coyote has much experience hunting pronghorns.

It appeared that tiny herds of pronghorns survived on much of their range. They were seen briefly at some distance, only to disappear into the countless gullies, coulees, mesas and hills of the prairie. Early in the 20th century, these few tenacious holdouts drew the attention of a budding wildlife conservation movement. Bison, being more promising, attracted entrepreneurs who hoped to profit from bison they owned. They were disappointed, but were able to unload their bison onto national governments that became active in conservation rather late. In a sense, business and government — big brothers — stepped in to save the bison. In the case of the pronghorn, it was more of a populist movement that flared up, probably independently in many localities, to save the remnants of the pronghorn herds. If there was a coordinated action across North America, it is a secret. Regionally, however, there are plenty of records of local people involved in saving pronghorns. Was this in response to a big case of bad conscience that rightly swept North America? Whatever the cause, if big brother buffalo was saved by big brothers, little brother pronghorn was saved by little brothers.

Although today some ranchers cuss the pronghorn as a stinky goat and would like to see less, few ranchers realize how much effort, goodwill and money went into bringing the pronghorn back from the edge of extinction. Much of that effort came from civic-minded landowners and fledgling game departments. Although the bison's fate, unfortunately, still hangs in the air, pronghorns have assumed a role as a tolerable nuisance on private ranches and public highways. They cause little damage and do a lot of good.

It came about as part of a greater miracle: the continental surge of activity to conserve dwindling natural resources, in particular, wildlife. This movement began just before or during World War I at a meeting between the United States and Canada, fostered by President Teddy Roosevelt and Prime Minister Sir Wilfred Laurier. Public debate led to legislation in both countries and the first international wildlife treaties. These treaties worked. It is too bad that the terrible calamity of the Great War obscured what became the greatest environmental success story of the 20th century. It was the finest system of wildlife conservation ever, the only large-scale system of sustainable natural resource development, a great contributor to the quality of life in North America, and a howling economic success in which private enterprise profited from a public resource. Ironically, this public good was the brainchild of some of the foremost capitalist entrepreneurs at the turn of the century such as Sir Clifford Sifton, a multimillionaire and the brain behind the development of the Canadian West. For nearly a decade — from 1911 to 1919 — Sifton ran Canada's Commission on Conservation. His counterpart in the United States was the great Gifford Pinchot.

E X P O S E D

species for posterity, it needs
to native plants, climates and predators.

North America's wildlife conservation system is ingenious! It is managed to captivate the enthusiasm and support of the common person — blue-collar workers and rural people who have been paying dearly for environmental protection for decades without knowing it. Although it was the successful brainchild of a social elite, it never became a symbol of an intellectual urban elite who is uncaring toward the common person, as have environmental and animal-rights movements. Wildlife conservation returned most species from the edge of extinction, increased wildlife abundance continually over 80 years, gave rise to the profession of public wildlife manager, organized citizens into myriad conserva-

tion organizations, and taxed the users of wildlife on behalf of wildlife. It is a success story, a great achievement that North Americans should rightly be proud of. Too bad it is also the best-kept secret. Too bad most take wildlife for granted, having never learned of the work and anguish that people in the past experienced so our generation might enjoy wildlife.

As to pronghorns, their abundance is not only a consequence of decades of protection, but of hands-on management, in particular, of active reintroductions to abandoned pronghorn ranges. Like mountain sheep, small relict pronghorn populations have difficulty growing and expanding. One can protect

BOTH SEXES ARE present in this fleeing herd. The bucks have dropped their horn sheaths.

Are you surprised by that question? If so, you might ask it more often! You might discover that an initial act of kindness — this act of conservation, this matter of the heart — returns hard benefits for us. Wildlife conservation is not a one-way street nor a mere exercise in environmental ethics. It is a good, proven way to look after our own interests. Conservation means jobs, wealth, health, utility, prosperity, enjoyment and longevity for us the conservers! Conservation stands for the good life — our good life. And pronghorns, like all wildlife species, pay us back handsomely indeed.

The pronghorn pays us back in two ways. First, it opens up ecosystems that, without pronghorns, are closed to us. The pronghorn converts myriad poisonous plants, which our livestock species cannot use, into meat, recreation and an economy based on these. To eat pronghorn is to eat converted sage, cacti and creosote bush, just as to eat trout is to eat converted earthworms, grasshoppers and caddis flies. To some grossly overfed, intellectually lazy urbanites, this is a matter of political incorrectness. However, to those who have suffered hardship and hunger, who had ample cause to think about where their daily food comes from, this is no trivial matter. Every species we save can convert part of the biota into something useful for humans. Vulgar, isn't it? I relish such vulgarity!

Let's have a little more of this vulgarity. Here is a

and sit and wait for populations to grow, and one can wait a long, long time. Some relict herds did expand a little, but by and large such was paltry. It was the capture and redistribution of pronghorns that finally did the trick, of which much occurred between 1925 and 1944. This movement happened across the pronghorn's range from Alberta to Texas and from California to Oklahoma as concerned conservationists decided on reintroductions and carried them out. That did it. By the 1980s, pronghorns numbered close to a million. It's not all peaches and cream, but it does seem that pronghorns are back to stay, which is living proof that conservation works.

And what in return has the pronghorn done for us?

link of pronghorns to humans via utility, a material — not a philosophical, ethical or romantic — bond. Yet it is material bonds that endure, that unite humans — who are so engaged in work for the partner on the other side of the relationship — with, in this instance, pronghorns. If one can add romantic, ethical and philosophical links, so much the better. However, such are but the icing on the cake. Romance, ethics and philosophy are of little value when the chips are down without the material link. The link of greatest value is always the material link between locals and valued aspects of the environment. That is one lesson arising from North America's system of wildlife conservation. Fortunately, it is also an idea that is being pushed globally by conservation organizations.

Yes, pronghorns provide good meat, usually, but not always. Some rutting bucks can be raunchy. Does this mean that because the meat is usually good one should domesticate pronghorns so their meat can be bought at the grocery store? Not at all. That is a certain way to destroy pronghorns. Domestication is the deliberate destruction of natural adaptations to make the beasts tractable and produce most what the market desires. So far, pronghorns have escaped the grasp of agriculture. Elk, bison and white-tailed deer have not been so lucky. Nor have pronghorns been the focus of another destructive trend, that of trophy production. Moreover, putting wildlife behind fences or in cages generates less wealth for society than letting them run free.

Turn pronghorns over to private hands, and the public loses its interest and its ability to watch over the species. No, pronghorns do best in the public domain, the domain that has returned them from oblivion at public expense. By granting a legal harvest — and the use of the word *harvest* is correct and appropriate here — under professional care with political responsibility going back to elected representatives, one ensures the continued material, but also emotional bond of those willing to hunt. And, it's public, in the open, and accessible to all — righteous meddlers included.

They are an inseparable part of the system, and quite essential to its success, just so long as they remain vigorous watchdogs and not more. They need not be right all the time as watchdogs to keep politicians and bureaucrats on their toes and accountable. And this needs to be done.

We also get paid by pronghorns and other wildlife via the abundant economic activities they ignite. The North American economy based on wildlife is akin to that based on automobiles. Both make inefficiency a virtue, in that inefficiencies create wealth and employment. Cars are an inefficient mode of transportation, but a highly convenient and appealing one. It is similar with our wildlife economy. For instance, you cannot do the efficient thing to enjoy a robin, by caging it and having it sing in your home. That's against the law. You may, however, enjoy robins by getting out of your house in an appropriate

dress and heading for where robins happen to be singing. That means you buy proper clothing, boots, binoculars, bird guide, transportation and food during the outing. That's legal, but inefficient and costly, and is called bird-watching. In a similar vein, you may catch trout the arduous, inefficient and expensive way by means of a dry fly, rather than the efficient way of a stick of dynamite thrown into a river pool. In a similar vein, it costs much more to hunt and eat a pronghorn than to buy the same amount of beef or lamb in a store. The hunting of pronghorns under North American rules is horrendously inefficient and expensive. One must pay for license, equipment, transportation, camping fees, motel and restaurant costs, which add up fast. There are about 30 pounds of meat on a pronghorn buck, less on a doe. A pronghorn's meat is equivalent to about $80, but the most frugal of hunts will still cost $350 to

$400 per pronghorn. It costs even more by the time the meat is cut, wrapped and frozen and the refrigerator or freezer is paid for. Wild meat — good as it is nutritionally — is certainly no bargain!

Viewers of pronghorn, collectively, pay even more. However, studies in Wyoming — where most pronghorns are found — indicate that most wildlife viewers — people who make a special effort to come and watch pronghorns in spring and summer — are hunters and their families. When everything is added together by all involved, viewers and hunters, the amount of economic activity per living pronghorn generated in Wyoming exceeded $1,000 annually. That's a staggering amount. These figures are now almost a decade old, but I doubt that watching and hunting pronghorns today is any cheaper than it was a decade ago. Figures from the 1990s indicate that the United States generates a first-time spending

DEC

on wildlife and fish of almost $60 billion annually, or more than $16,500 per square mile. About 50,000 jobs are created for every billion dollars input. Wildlife pays through its nose for its existence!

A review of the figures indicates that wealth is created from wildlife by the number of people participating in wildlife-related activities, and not by the amount paid per person. Thus, visitors of modest means who come to hunt, who make it a vacation, who explore on their own, spend on average more money for every animal they kill than do affluent individuals who hire guides and hunt areas denied to the public. Is that not ironic? When wildlife is restricted for the enjoyment of the rich elite, as it might well be if matters continue as they are, then a wealth-creating public good will be lost. In addition, there will be no reason or incentive for the public to be interested in wildlife, as is the case in much of western Europe today. This opens the way to the abuse of wildlife as happened historically with boring regularity when ownership slipped from the public into private hands. Now that wildlife has been restored in North America, largely at public expense, now that it has become valuable, there will be no shortage of entrepreneurs trying to convince politicians that conservation is better served by wildlife in private hands. Public beware!

Of course, the pronghorn pays back in more than material wealth and meat. It is a strikingly beautiful animal, a decoration of the prairie, something to lighten the monotony of many miles of wheat deserts. A territorial pronghorn buck posing on a hill in evening light is a striking picture. Pronghorn kids racing across the prairie are a wonder to behold. The pronghorn also instructs us in its biology about adaptations to the past and its way of coping today. As long as it graces the prairie, we will gain new insights and be thrilled and awed by the intricacies of nature's way. The pronghorn is a living monument to the many good men and women who worked without reward so pronghorns might live, so future generations might enjoy the little racer of the prairies. How can one ever repay those good people long in their graves?

As to the future, it is by no means certain. A review of the past reveals that conservation was always in crisis. Presumably, it always will be. What is new about history is the insight that in the past eight decades, North Americans built a wildlife conservation system without peer. It is an open public system, one beset by tedious, absurd, boring, trivial, but also profound and wise arguments that characterize the democratic process. It is precisely that every voice is heard, no matter how unreasonable and absurd, that voices of wisdom and insight are also heard. Democracy is a protection from extremes. The fate of those hired by the public to manage wildlife carry a heavy burden and have much frustration to face. Normally, these individuals are unaware just how great their contribution is to the quality of life we enjoy through our wildlife. They only note that when they do something right, nobody remembers, and when they do something wrong, nobody forgets. However, that's the nature of democracy. Its redeeming feature is that it ultimately works. History teaches that wildlife, in the long term, is looked after best by this messy democratic system as a public good. As long as that is the case, the pronghorn is safe.

CHAPTER 8

THE HUNT AND AFTER

The quality of wild meat is nutritionally superior. Its taste is highly variable, much of a treat, but occasionally a bust. And that's where a little know-how comes in.

PRAIRIE

Dawn was breaking on the frosty prairie

The payoff in wildlife conservation is, ultimately, a very personal matter. The sound of migrating geese overhead, the busy squabbles of colorful mallard drakes and hens as they embark on next year's marital affairs, the bugling of bull elk resounding in the moon-lit valley, a grizzly bear mother reclining in a mountain stream as her cubs splash in the water, or a herd of pronghorns on the deep green of the awakening prairie. These and other sights I cannot do without. However, there is another wildlife matter I do not want to miss: the exquisite food that wildlife provides through hunting. The quality of wild meat, taken and processed with due care, is nutritionally superior because of its high protein and vitamin content. Its taste is highly variable, much of it a treat, but occasionally a bust. And that's where a little know-how comes in.

Dawn was breaking on the frosty prairie. The first rays of the sun played on the peaks of Wyoming's Bighorn Ranges to the west. My first day of pronghorn hunting lay ahead, and hope burnt in my chest that I would see a fine buck somewhere out there in the wide flats. It was toward the end of the season, the only time I could go hunting. A distant herd of pronghorns came into view, but they were far away. Then movement caught my eye low on a ridge — a pair of pronghorns, a female and fawn, the female limping. That terminated any scanning for bucks. I had a couple of doe-fawn licenses in my pocket, one of the benefits of Wyoming's

good management. Pronghorns are abundant and in need of annual cropping, which can only be done by annually reducing the female and fawn population. My licenses were thus applicable to that unfortunate pair. I cannot say I was pleased at the prospect of tagging a wounded doe, but there is really no choice in the matter, as the culling of wounded game is a hunter's first duty. Well before the sunlight had reached the ridge, the doe and fawn disappeared. My first task was to find them. Where would they be?

A wounded pronghorn that is aware of a pur-

EARLY MORNING light on female harem in rut.

suing hunter is virtually uncatchable, because it detects the pursuer and flees at incredible distances. One always sees the quarry jumping up in unexpected locations and disappearing quickly over a distant rise. A pronghorn that is not alerted to a pursuer, however, will hide. Where? In hilly country, such as the foothills of the Bighorns, it will invariably be somewhere high and close to rocks or clumps of sage — in a draw, in a small depression or flat spot on a ridge crest, or in a clump of sage close to the ridgeline. Moreover, when seeing a hunter, such pronghorns tend to hold in hiding and might

startle the unprepared with their sudden eruption from cover and speedy departure.

I suspected the wounded doe would hide on the ridge below where I had spotted her. I thus climbed that ridge and proceeded slowly along the top, looking for depressions that could hide a pronghorn. The wounded doe jumped up about 100 paces in front of me from a hiding place beside a small rock outcrop in a coulee. Two quick shots killed her and the fawn. Had this been a normal hunt for meat, I would

probably have shot only the fawn. Pronghorn fawns are large in fall, but are nevertheless severely threatened by the coming winter, and thus the best class of pronghorns to cull. Moreover, their meat is usually superlative.

I stepped up to the doe with some trepidation. She had a fresh wound low in the left haunch that caused her limping. Fortunately, I soon discovered that only meant a little less meat because the rest of the carcass revealed a healthy animal. I had no worry the meat would be good.

Now, pronghorn meat is not always good, but then, neither is that of other game. I have eaten wonderful moose meat, and I have had raunchy moose meat, ditto for elk, deer, rabbits, caribou, mallards, mountain goats, mountain sheep and Canada geese. There are situations when one need not bother killing an animal because it will not be good or safe to eat, such as old, gaunt bull moose in winter, caribou or mountain goats in rut, mallards that have switched from feeding on grains to feeding on invertebrates on ice-free rivers, snowshoe hares sitting about apathetically and close to death during highs in their population cycles, and bears that have feasted on spawning salmon, carrion or garbage dumps. In the latter case, the concern is not only for foul-tasting meat or foul-smelling carcasses, but also for the threat of trichinosis. Rabbits are normally fine, but a quick check of the liver for tiny yellow lines is in order. It might be caused by harmless coccidia or by dangerous tularaemia. In either case, a quick washing of the hands is in order. Clearly, if one wants good meat on the table, one must have some appropriate knowledge. But then, the same holds true when collecting any wild food in the forest and field, be it salads, berries — and in particular — mushrooms.

One element affecting the meat's taste is the food habits of the game. If the feed is diverse vegetation low in secondary plant compounds, the meat is likely to be the best. Consequently,

N T

I prefer to collect meat early in fall, preferably at higher elevations where meadows are late to bloom, or in lowlands where big game feed extensively in alfalfa fields, on winter-wheat or late-cut meadows. Meat from game that is short of food because of competition, which consequently overbrowses woody vegetation, is likely to have an unpleasant, even bitter taste because of an excessive intake of secondary plant compounds — a fancy word for plant toxins. These appear to accumulate in meat and fat. I can taste when deer in late-fall have switched from dried and cured forbs to woody browse by the slight bittering of the meat, and I do not like it! Pronghorns from dense populations, which have little else to feed on than sparse native prairie, and which might then feed heavily on sage, acquire a sage-like taste. That is definitely not for every palate, including mine. However, that can be remedied splendidly with appropriate cooking skills. Nevertheless, I prefer to hunt game that is not

BUCKS, AFTER INITIALLY joining does in large herds in early winter, soon segregate into small bachelor groups that move about on their own.

forced onto a starvation diet. You never need to worry about pronghorn meat taken from thriving, low-expanding populations, particularly if they dwell on rich, productive soils covered by a species-rich flora. And that applied to the wounded doe and the fawn I had killed. That's the main reason I had no worries about the meat. The healing wound in the female's haunch was no cause for concern. All that was needed was to cut out the damaged portions. The rest of the meat would be fine.

I proceeded to cool the meat quickly, and dress out the animals so as not to dirty the meat with soil, grit, dust, urine, plant debris, glandular secretions or gut-content. Because I would need to carry the pronghorns but a short distance to a nearby vehicle trail, I could afford to open up the animals maximally to let the heat

forms a protective skin over exposed muscle meat.

Skin the two animals? Not till final butchering. The skin is needed to keep the meat clean, moist and unaffected by spoilage. With so small an animal as a pronghorn, taken on a frosty October morning, the meat will cool quickly even with the skin. That's, of course, not true for elk and moose killed in hot weather, where the skin must come off at once and the animal must be dismantled — even stuck into a cold mountain stream, in the shade — to facilitate cooling. I next carried the two carcasses into the shadow of a north-facing cliff where I did not expect the sun to reach all day. Here I spread the carcasses to facilitate cooling. I left my sweaty undershirt dangling above the meat to keep away coyotes. In the evening, the pronghorns would be hung up in the shade where the cold night breezes could thoroughly chill them.

Some hang meat for aging, claiming that it tenderizes and improves flavor. I do not. I skin, cut up the meat and try to get it frozen as soon as possible. To each his own! Freezing also tenderizes the meat, and there is no chance for off-tastes to develop. The two pronghorns were cut up, frozen and wrapped within two days, and that's how they made the long journey to Canada. A good part of the wounded haunch was saved. The loss of meat was negligible.

With the carcasses cooling and secured against coyotes, I resumed hunting. I took an old, regressing pronghorn buck a day later.

escape. That is, I could proceed with the classical European way of dressing, by opening up the neck from the head to the brisket, removing the trachea and knotting the gullet so no rumen content would spill. Female pronghorns have no foul-smelling glandular secretions to the exterior, or urine-soaked hairs that one must avoid touching. Gutting was quickly completed, and a clean carcass lay before me. I made sure the interior was washed out with the blood that had accumulated in the thoracic cavity. The blood quickly

CHAPTER 9

HOW TO TAME A GAMEY BUCK

Unlike this yearling buck, old rutting bucks can be foul-tasting. The taste causes some to stop hunting, while others patiently stew, spice and suffer through every inedible shot. However, a few tricks can erase the gamey taste of a rutting buck.

Three fine pronghorn bucks lay outside the tent. We had been successful as well as lucky. In Alberta, antelope licenses are distributed by drawing, and you have to be lucky to be chosen. My friend Ron, my two boys and I had drawn permits. We had planned the hunt well and, on the morning of the first day, Ron and the boys had shot fine bucks. I took a large buck on the second morning.

We were in camp at dusk on the first evening. We were tired, happy and very hungry. As always, after killing any big-game animal, I had kept the livers, hearts and kidneys. I sliced one liver and dusted the pieces with flour, pepper and salt. The heavy skillet was hot, and a generous lump of fresh butter was melting in it. Soon, the slices were sizzling in the bubbling butter. Quickly, I got out the sourdough bread and cut it up. This would not be a fancy meal, just sound fare for hungry mouths. The liver was quickly fried, and I distributed the slices. Then, I turned to fry a second batch.

An odd sound made me turn around. A less-than-happy expression distorted everyone's face.

"Anything wrong?" I asked.

"It's a bit strong," Ron said with a gulp.

"Yeech," was the comment from Karl.

"Dad, you better try some yourself," said Harold, my youngest.

Abandoning the frying pan, I reached for my plate and bit into the first piece of buck antelope liver that I had ever tasted. Phew! Awful! Filthy! Had I ever bitten into anything as ghastly before? Nothing equaled this liver taste. It was as if I had sunk my teeth into the hairy, oily rotting gland that each antelope buck carries below his ears — the black spot just behind the hinge of the jaw that produces secretions used to mark territory. This was no sage taste in my mouth. The sage taste is bearable, the rutting taste of antelope is not.

I grabbed the frying pan and flung the liver slices into the ravine. "May the coyote make a feast of it, or the badger, or the bobcat, or whomever," I thought.

As I looked over those sleek, beautiful antelope bucks, my mind filled with foreboding. It turned out that the meat of all three bucks had a penetrating, horrible rutting taste. Harold's buck, a fine 14-inch-

er, was almost edible. Karl's buck, an old, regressed fighter with 11-inch horns and a broken fork, was the worst. The buck had a gaunt body covered with bruises from a fight. To make matters worse, Karl's first shot had drifted off target because of the strong prairie wind and had hit the gut. After Karl killed the buck, he discovered he had lost his knife and had to run some miles to camp to get another one. Meanwhile, the contents of the gut soaked the meat. My own buck, a large-bodied, fat fellow with heavy 14½-inch horns, had been hit lengthwise and low. I cleaned the carcass at once, and yet the meat was

almost as foul-tasting as Karl's buck. This was all the worse, because the meat was tender, had a beautiful texture and contained relatively little fat. Chemical analysis shows that antelope meat is higher in protein, vitamins and minerals than beef.

Mountain goat billies killed in the rut have meat that, when cooked, exudes a filthy odor and tastes horrible. I had experienced that, but the antelope meat from our hunt surpassed even goat meat. What was I to do? In our family, the rule is: If you kill it, you clean it and eat it. If you do not want to eat it, you simply do not kill it.

The sage taste is bearable, the rutting taste of antelope

After butchering the three bucks, I hauled 30 pounds of meat to a local Austrian butcher. He added beef shank and pork and made classical German bratwurst or frying sausage. To my surprise, it turned out excellent. In fact, that was the best batch of sausage he made for us that year. I would have gladly brought all the antelope meat to him, but, by then, it was in the freezer. To make frying sausage, fresh meat is required. Anyway, we had more than enough elk and moose sausage already.

When in doubt, call friends. Only then did I discover that foul-tasting antelope is not uncommon. Some of my acquaintances had quit hunting antelope on that account. Others continued hunting, celebrated every edible antelope, and spiced, stewed and suffered through every other one. Nobody in my immediate circle of acquaintances knew how to deal with foul-tasting antelope meat. I had a problem.

The first roast I cooked like hasenpfeffer — hare stew in a vinegar marinade. I marinated the meat in a mixture of dark stout and wine vinegar, with plenty of fresh onions and black pepper. It didn't work. Next, I tried a soy-sauce marinade on lean slices of antelope meat, and I stir-fried them in a wok. That didn't work.

I boiled the hearts in a rich mixture of garden herbs and vegetables. It was awful! Next, I cooked the tongues in sour cream. Horrible! After hearing of my plight, a Swiss colleague recommended buttermilk as a marinade. He had used it on antelope with good results. Off I rushed and bought two liters of buttermilk. For seven long days, I marinated antelope steaks in buttermilk. It didn't work.

I made a terrine de pate, which is French for meat loaf. I used ground pork for half of the meat, and I doubled the amount of brandy and went a bit heavy on spices. The terrine was rather snappy. I served it at a party, and the adults liked it. The taste of the rut was gone, but the children detested my terrine. They said the brandy was overpowering. Scratch that one! The meat loaf was not family fare.

Next, I took some thin steaklets, rubbed mustard over them, rolled them in fine bread crumbs, black pepper and salt, and fried them crisp. With the meat, I served a spicy white sauce — just in case. My wife liked the dish. I could still taste buck.

At a downtown talk I gave, I met a lady who had a long acquaintance with the ways of American Indians. Antelope? Why yes, some can be quite gamey, but a few days of marinating in tomato juice will cure that, she told me. That's how her Indian friends treated antelope. Tomato juice? People use it to deodorize clothes and dogs that have been sprayed by skunks. Maybe it would work. Eagerly, I headed home and marinated a roast for three days in tomato juice. It didn't work.

I'd have to consult game cookbooks. Off I went in search of antelope recipes, but pronghorns are conspicuously absent from cookbooks. I

ABLE

is not.

finally found one recipe, but it had obviously been concocted for nongamey antelope meat because it treated the meat like bland veal.

At that point, I remembered Schroeder. I had seen my friend Schroeder in Italy the previous summer. We were at a conference on mountain ungulates, hoofed mammals such as gorals, serow, chamois, wild sheep and mountain goats. Dr. Wolfgang Schroeder is head of the Wildlife Institute at the University of Munich in Germany, and like me, is an avid hunter and cook. Dr. Schroeder mentioned a marinade used by backwoods residents of the Alps to make rutting chamois bucks edible. Schroeder had used it on ibex buck, which can be exceptionally filthy. A rutting ibex buck is reputed to smell and taste like an uncastrated billy goat, only worse. Because I have shot many feral goats, some big billies included, I had an inkling of what rutting ibex would taste like.

A friend in need is a friend indeed! Schroeder wasted no time. Within a few days — bless the postal service — I had his letter in hand. Not only had he written down the recipe for the marinade, but he also included several ways to prepare rutting ibex or chamois meat. Would this time-tested marinade work on rutting pronghorns, too? It did, but only when the meat was braised — browned in fat and simmered in a covered pan with liquid. The results were so good that even my finicky kids ate it. They were actually grieved when the meat was gone, and they were eager to apply for another hunt! If this recipe will work on rutting antelope, it will work on any strong-tasting game you might shoot.

Marinade Schroeder

You need one quart of red wine. I prefer a heavy full-bodied dry wine. Add one quart of fresh orange juice. Schroeder used apple cider or apple juice. Both work fine, but I prefer orange juice. Add one 6-ounce cup of wine vinegar. No ordinary cider vinegar, please! Add a handful of juniper berries, about 25. I collect mine from the prostrate juniper in the foothills, but the common juniper will do. Add one handful of whole cloves, about 25, two bay leaves, and four medium carrots that have been scraped and shredded. Do not add salt!

Bring the ingredients to a boil, reduce heat, and let the mixture simmer 15 minutes. I use an enameled steel pot — no aluminum, please. Let the marinade cool, and add the antelope meat. Store in a cool place for at least two days, but there's no harm in keeping it in the marinade for up to seven days. If you use apple cider or juice instead of orange juice, the marinade will turn cloudy by the second day. That's a good sign — it means the marinade is working. This marinade draws the albumen out of the meat, which appears as scum when you boil meat or bones for stock. This scum must be skimmed off and discarded.

The marinade can be used for a second batch but not for a third. To use it a second time, bring the marinade to a boil and remove the thick albumen scum. Taste the marinade. You might have to adjust the taste with a shot of port wine or brandy. After the second use, I've found the marinade is no longer usable because it tastes like antelope buck, even after the albumen scum is removed.

Marinating the meat, however, is only half the battle. With thick chunks of meat, even seven days of marinating will not remove the deep-sealed buck taste. You must also braise the meat. That is, cook the meat so the fibers rupture and allow the deep juices to seep out and the braising liquid to seep in.

You exchange tissue juice for braising liquid. Properly braised meat is tender. The following two recipes are both braises.

Antelope Alberta

Drain the marinated 3- to 4-pound roast thoroughly, and remove as much surface moisture as possible. If need be, use a towel. Set the meat aside. Use a ceramic pot that will just barely hold the roast and vegetables. There shouldn't be any space between the meat and sides of the pot.

To prepare the vegetable bed, clean and cut into chunks six medium carrots, one large parsnip and one large onion.

In a pan, melt fresh butter and add a little olive oil. Add salt and sugar. I use about a half-teaspoon each, but a little extra sugar doesn't hurt. Heat the vegetables gently in hot butter. Carefully watch them so they don't burn. Remove the browned vegetables and place them in the bottom of the ceramic pot. I use a crock pot because it is handy.

Now sear and brown the meat thoroughly. Yes, you must have a hard, brown crust. Do not stop until you get it. When the roast is finally browned all over, put it on top of the vegetables in the ceramic pot.

Thin a 4-ounce can of tomato paste with a splash of port wine or sherry. Brandy works fine, too, if you only have adults to feed! Add two heaping teaspoons of brown sugar to the diluted paste. Now stir, and pour the mixture over the roast. Add one uncrushed, large clove of garlic. Cover the pot and cook at 325 degrees. When using a crock pot, turn it on high and leave covered.

About one hour later, check to see if the meat has given off juice and has sunk into the pot. If not, continue until it does. Then pour some liquid in the pot over the meat and let simmer.

About two hours into the process, I taste the braising liquid and adjust with salt, lemon juice and brown sugar. If the liquid is too thin, I let the meat bubble without a lid until the juice has thickened, then I adjust the taste. Thereafter, I let the braise simmer. Five hours is good.

I recommend serving the meat with rice — wild rice mixed with brown rice is a festive addition. Also serve with a crisp salad and an aromatic, dry red wine. The taste resembles good barbecued beef.

Antelope for Hunters

Take 3 pounds of cubed antelope meat, and marinate it a la Schroeder. Dice a half-pound of good-quality bacon. Fry the bacon until it is crisp, and then put it into the pot. Use the remaining bacon fat to brown three large diced onions and two diced stalks of celery. Put them into the pot. Brown the antelope meat in small batches in the remaining bacon fat, to which I add a lump of butter. Put the meat in the pot and add one large, crushed garlic clove. I also like to add a generous handful of dried mushrooms. If you don't have dried mushrooms, fry a half-pound of meadow mushrooms in butter until brown. Next, brown three large tablespoons of flour in the remaining fat. You might have to add some butter to get a good brown roux. With a cup or two of lukewarm beef stock, make a sauce with black pepper and salt. Pour over meat and vegetables in the pot. Close the pot and turn on the heat. One hour later, adjust taste with salt and add two tablespoons of brandy — a little more doesn't hurt. Let the pot simmer. You can stir the ingredients a little. A beautiful, brown sauce should form.

Serve with broccoli, boiled fresh potatoes and fresh, crusty bread. Depending on the occasion, serve a dry red wine or some hearty ale or beer.

Antelope Westphalia

There is at least one more way to obtain a superb product from the gamiest antelope. Albumen gives meat the bad taste, and it can be extracted by salting. Rub coarse, noniodized salt into the meat to extract a lot of fluid in only 24 hours. Wash the meat thoroughly to remove the salt, and use an equal amount of ground pork in hamburger dishes. However, if you have a smoker, you can do as I did.

After 24 hours, drain and briefly rinse the meat. Make a paste with a half pound of brown sugar, 1 ounce of baking soda and 1 ounce of liquid Vitamin C. Pour it over the meat, and let stand in an earthenware pot in a cool place for four days. Turn the meat daily. Drain meat and let its surface dry. Place in a preheated smoker for 24 hours, keeping the heat low. The result is dark, shriveled meat, greatly reduced in size. On the inside, however, it is deep red and flavored like an old-time ham.

To our sorrow, the meat vanished too rapidly. Be it gamey or not, I am looking forward to my next antelope.

ADDITIONAL READING

Jim D.Yoakum and Bart W. O'Gara (2000) "Pronghorn," Chapter 23 pp. 559-577 in Stephen Demarais and Paul K. Krausman (eds.) *Ecology and Management of Large Mammals in North America*. Prentice Hall, Upper Saddle River, NJ 07458.
This writing features the most recent scientific summary of pronghorns. Both authors are seasoned biologists who have contributed greatly to our understanding of pronghorns. The book won an award from The Wildlife Society.

Jim D.Yoakum (1978) "Pronghorn." Chapter 7, pp. 103-121 in J.L. Schmidt and W. Schwartz (eds.) *Big Game of North America*. Stackpole Books, Harrisburg, Pa.
In this prize-winning book, Yoakum and O'Gara also present recent scientific studies about pronghorns. They are collaborating on a monograph on pronghorns to be published by the Wildlife Management Institute.

Arthur S. Einarsen, (1948) *The Pronghorn Antelope and its Management*. The Wildlife Management Inst. Washington, D.C., 238 pp.
Einarsen delivers a lively, often anecdotal, highly enjoyable account of the natural history of pronghorns and the struggle to re-establish and secure its population. Little did he know how successful these efforts would be.

John D. Caton (1877). *The Antelope and Deer of America*. Reprinted 1974 by Arno Press, New York. 426 pp.
Caton, a keen observer, kept deer and pronghorns in captivity and recorded significant detail firsthand. Please note: It is significant enough to have warranted reprinting!

John A. Byers (1997) *American Pronghorn*. University of Chicago Press, Chicago, 300 pp. Subtitle: "Social Adaptations and the Ghost of Predator's Past."
Byers picked up on the old idea that pronghorn biology is shaped by its history, foremost by predators now extinct. Much of the material is technical, but Byers writes well.

David W. Kitchen (1974). "Social behaviour and ecology of the pronghorn." *Wildlife Monographs* No. 38, 96 pp., George J. Mitchell (1980). *The Pronghorn Antelope in Alberta*. University of Regina. Saskatchewan. 165 pp.
Kitchen is an insightful young scientist. Mitchell summarizes his many years of work with pronghorns. Highly recommended!

Jim D.Yoakum and Don E. Spalding (1979) (eds.) "American Pronghorn Antelope" Articles published in the *Journal of Wildlife Management* 1937 to 1977. The Wildlife Society, Washington, D.C.
A fine collection of papers.

Bart W. O'Gara (1969). "Unique aspects of reproduction in the female pronghorn (*Antilocapra americana Ord*)" *American Journal of Anatomy* 125:217-232.

Bart W. O' Gara and G. Matson. 1975. "Growth and casting of horns by pronghorns and exfoliation of horns in bovids." *Journal of Mammalogy* 56:829-846.
Among the many scientific papers, these two are worth digging out for their sheer originality.

George C. Frison (1991) *Prehistoric Hunters of the High Plains*. Academic Press, San Diego.
Frison deciphers the role of pronghorns in the ancient hunting economy of native North Americans, but he does so in good part as an experimental, hands-on archaeologist. It's a thrill to read.

Peter T. Bromley (1977). *Aspects of the Behavioural Ecology and Sociobiology of the Pronghorn (Antilocapra americana)*. Doctoral Dissertation, Univ. of Calgary. 370 pp.
Peter Bromley was one of the keenest observers of pronghorns, and one of the most fertile, original minds. He was the first to discover territoriality in pronghorns. He deciphered the logic of horn-shedding and the pronghorn fawn's security strategy aimed at aerial predators. He unraveled the unique manner pronghorns use to hold and manage their territory before and during rut, and he tied together the pronghorn's ecology into a coherent pattern with its environment. Any of these are outstanding contributions, and so much more the pity that Peter Bromley published but sparsely. For any serious study of pronghorns, reading this seminal volume is a must!

ABOUT THE AUTHOR

Valerius Geist is professor emeritus of environmental sciences in the faculty of environmental design at the University of Calgary. He obtained a Ph.D. in zoology in 1966 from the University of British Columbia after a six-year study of the behavior of free-living mountain sheep.

In 1967, he wrote his first book, *Mountain Sheep*, which earned The Wildlife Society's 1972 book-of-the-year award. He then took a position at the University of Calgary, where he became the founding director of a graduate program in environmental science. He worked as professor, program director and associate dean for the next quarter-century.

Geist's research focused on environmental health issues, which soon encompassed the Ice Age-history and biology of humans. In 1978, this led to his most important publication, *Life Strategies, Human Evolution, Environmental Design. Toward a Biological Theory of Health.*

Wildlife conservation and management, in particular, wildlife conservation policy, also became an area of ongoing investigation. In 1999, Geist and Dale Toweill wrote *Return of Royalty*, a history of the recovery of mountain sheep, which is distributed by the Boone and Crockett Club.

Geist has written and coedited 15 books, and contributed more than 250 papers and articles. He also wrote more than 50 entries for 17 encyclopedias, and produced many short documentary films. His expertise has been used in the production of popular publications and films, including the National Geographic Society, the Canadian and British Broadcasting corporations and independent film producers. His latest technical book, *Deer of the World*, earned him his sixth book-of-the-year award.

Geist's wife, Renate, is a published translator, bacteriologist and teacher. They have three children and two grandchildren. He retired in 1995 and is now translating theoretical biology into practice. He loves to hunt, hike, fish, garden, brew and cook.

ACKNOWLEDGMENTS

I am grateful to my students who went afield to study pronghorns, Peter T. Bromley, Eldon H. Bruns, Randal D. Glaholt and Rick F. Courtnay; to Glen Means on whose ranch I enjoyed great hospitality; to the Canadian Forces Military at the Suffield Military Reserve for their support; and to my colleagues, in particular Bart W. O'Gara, who read this manuscript, but above all was unstinting in his support and always available for discussions. There were many colleagues, students, officers and ranchers whom I encountered along the pronghorn trail over the years. They willingly or unwittingly contributed to my appreciation of the "last American." I recall them every so often and am grateful for their generosity of spirit. Over the years my wife, Renate, was always there with support, insights and critique, without which, this book would not be.

ABOUT THE PHOTOGRAPHER

Michael H. Francis, born in Maine, has spent the past 30 years as a resident of Montana. Mike is a graduate of Montana State University. Before becoming a full-time photographer, he worked in Yellowstone National Park for 15 seasons.

Michael's photography has been internationally recognized for its beautiful and informative nature imagery. His work has been published by the National Geographic Society, The Audubon Society, The National Wildlife Federation, and *Deer & Deer Hunting*, *Field & Stream* and *Outdoor Life* magazines, among others.

His photographs appear in more than 15 books, including *Track of the Coyote*, *Mule Deer Country*, *Elk Country*, *Wild Sheep Country* and *Moose*. *Pronghorn Country* is the fifth book Francis and Geist have collaborated on.

Mike lives in Billings, Mont., with his wife, Tori, and daughters, Elizabeth and Emily.

STAFF FOR THIS BOOK

Patrick Durkin	*Editor*
Jennifer A. Pillath	*Managing Editor*
Allen West	*Designer*